Transforming Inner City Evangelism:

For When You Care

Michael V. Fariss

Published by Urban Discovery Ministries, Inc.
P.O. Box 6381, Norfolk, Virginia 23508
www.urbandiscovery.org

Library of Congress Control Number: 2005937632

All Scripture quotations, unless otherwise noted, are taken from the King
James Version of the Bible. Those marked NIV are taken for the *Holy
Bible, New International Version*®. *NIV*®. Copyright © 1973, 1978, 1984
by International Bible Society. Used by permission of Zondervan. All
rights reserved.

The use of materials from various Web sites does not imply endorsement
of those sites in their entirety.

Printed in the United States of America

To Kim, Rebekah, Brent, Joanna and Katelyn

With gratitude to Rebekah Fariss, Greg Johnston, Deborah Leseberg, Sharon Michael, Peggy Pollara, Margo Taylor, Ken Watson and Denise Woodson who gave me feedback and who live out this book's principles.

For evangelists who long to equip and mobilize God's people for the spiritual harvest.

Contents

Preface

You are a few pages from experiencing a strategic planning process that exalts Jesus Christ as the Lord of the inner city spiritual harvest. While following His directive in Luke 10:2 to pray for laborers, I put in writing four practical steps for preparing evangelical Christians to become successful laborers in the inner city.

I aim to assist those whom God is raising up in churches and Christian schools who care about the plight of the poor, especially those in the inner city, and who seek direction on how to begin making lasting differences through Christ.

Success in this endeavor depends on whether you embrace this cause as a core value of your ministry. Please prayerfully receive hard-nose challenges that I make from Jesus' teachings. I invite you to join other concerned Christians in entering a bold new phase of evangelism leadership as you progress through this book's strategic planning.

Many African-American theologians have been trying to tell white evangelicals for a long time that our faith and practices fall short of fulfilling Christ's Great Commission in our own backyards. Since the Civil Rights Movement, they have achieved the freedom and opportunity to open their case against white evangelicals' beliefs and behaviors. By comparing Rick Warren's conclusions from his recent best selling book, *The Purpose-Driven® Life,* with criticisms from these African-Americans leaders, I question whether we missed mercy and justice in our quests to fulfill Christ's purposes.

I also include an inventory at the end of each chapter to

help churches, Christian schools, outreach ministries and individuals start strategic thinking that prevents Satan from discrediting the wonderful Gospel of Jesus. Other authors have warned that this kind of introspection might bring whites grieving with responses of anger, denial and sorrow.[1] Nevertheless, painful introspection provides an important transitional step for white persons who need to break away from racist tendencies, especially when given tools for constructive action.[2] I attempt to expose institutional and cultural racism in evangelical Christianity to begin "shaking the foundations on which our racialization is built."[3]

In this effort I risk isolating myself from my natural allies (and supporters) among liberals and conservatives. Readers with theologically liberal perspectives who share my passion for mercy and justice will undoubtedly disagree with conservative biblical assumptions that I present as indisputable. On the other hand I strongly criticize evangelicals' neglectful, racist and divisive structures.

Both sides acutely need strategic, practical ways to relationally and intentionally evangelize their neighbors through a verbal witness for Christ as they show true mercy. Therefore, I take seriously this opportunity to speak prophetically. I appeal to God's people to receive my assessments and join me in the inner city harvest for the sake of Jesus Christ and His Gospel.

Since some liberals call on evangelicals to end silence about social neglect, perhaps they will accept the reality that I must speak for mercy and justice from our doctrinally conservative framework when I heed their admonitions. I affirm the significance of all people, not judging them as good or bad, while relying on God's Word to distinguish right from wrong or truth from error.

My challenges in these chapters weigh heavy on my mind when I relate to inner city families during the course of my ministry. They especially impact young men who experience the alienating consequences of our sins that destroy their faith in our Lord. Those who have suffered from injustices would probably say that my words still remain too soft. May the Lord of the harvest, nevertheless, use these pages to somehow thrust out workers for the inner city.

To further this cause, please prayerfully prepare for new critical thinking about how to live purpose-driven® as I address evangelical Christians' past and present evangelism and church growth strategies. Wanting to speak the truth in love, I explain how the Evil One still uses sins from the past to undermine the credibility of the Gospel in the inner city. Our repentance must include honestly recognizing and tearing down spiritual strongholds that have gone up during past generations and currently work against the purposes of God, as we now accept responsibility for evangelizing our inner cities through mercy and justice ministries as explained in Chapter 15.

One of the goals of this book is to provide practical insights into how to wage urban spiritual warfare and overcome the devil's attempts to prevent our bold, clear witness for Christ in the inner city. I conclude with a practical project from Luke 10 that can help churches or outreach ministries launch long-term relational community evangelism.

This book's principles come from an evangelist seeking to equip those whom God would thrust out into the spiritual harvest. Without the benefit of an agricultural background, Jesus' farming illustration in Luke 10 may not seem relevant in the inner city.

However, the Lord's directive to pray that He thrust out

much needed workers for a plentiful spiritual harvest can apply directly to the inner city. Therefore, read on for Jesus' transferable, timeless and vital principles for the mobilization of workers for the harvest of evangelism in today's inner city environment. By working through this chapter in the Bible, I define true mercy and explain how God wants to make it our priority.

I trust that this book will elevate the role of evangelists in developing spiritual legacies in the inner city. Although many in Hampton Roads had small family gardens in the past, few still exist in downtown Norfolk. Most gardens disappeared, lacking a legacy of younger workers to sustain them. After directing for eight years an outreach center for inner city young people, I organized an evangelistic tent crusade in their neighborhood to combat the destructive advent of "crack" cocaine there. I placed a large blue-stripped tent next to a garden that a retired grandmother cultivated on land where the Housing Authority had torn down and removed blocks of slum houses. After a grueling week of preparation for this crusade, followed by nine days of spiritual warfare and power, our team of urban missionaries baptized eight adults in a neighborhood swimming pool.

While I could have felt quite satisfied with these results, Sarah Pilcher, a godly widow and one of our prayer partners, approached me under the tent at the end of the crusade and remarked, "You know that you haven't finished the work until you equip these converts to reach their community." In one sentence she commissioned me in the biblical, but often forgotten, role of an evangelist, "to prepare God's people for works of service" (Eph. 4:12). Heeding her challenge resulted in the development of the principles described in this book. I believe that spiritually gifted evangelists have important responsibilities in Christ's work of thrusting out laborers.

I also address questions that some middle class believers ask me about ministering to inner city families of different races or socio-economic backgrounds. Knowing that God works through local churches in the harvest, I seek spiritual opportunities to equip and mobilize them for urban evangelism. Although white Christians may feel uncomfortable with my direct challenges to them, let me confirm that I appreciate our important roles and responsibilities in the spiritual harvest in the inner city.

Many evangelicals live in the "Red States" where they attend church regularly, appreciate Biblical teaching and sacrificially protect their families from ungodly influences. Although they value love for God, neighbors and country, for reasons that I will explain later many in society label them with this red color as extremists, ignorant, unreasonable, cold, materialistic, racist, self-centered, and right-wing fundamentalists. They probably feel hurt by these accusations and confused by the political and social issues related to inner city life. Yet some still care about the poor and have already become connected with people who live in poverty. As they seek answers about how to begin to make a lasting difference, I offer insights to help them respond to Christ's Great Commission.

Throughout the book, I show how extending mercy as Jesus commanded is a necessary and effective requirement for successful evangelism, regardless of race. Christians often include a broad range of outreaches to the poor when thinking of mercy and justice ministries in general terms. In Chapter 15, I clarify the meanings of these words in Scripture and show how some outreaches, though benevolent, do not fulfill Christ's command to love our neighbors.

To readers of African descent, I ask for grace. Please

remember, before you go on, the great testimony for Christ of your faithful willingness to forgive.

For persons of other races or from different ethnic backgrounds, I request your patience as I focus on the black/white issues undermining the credibility of our witness for Christ. I certainly appreciate your important roles in inner city and worldwide harvest fields.

I have prayed that the Lord will thrust the readers of this book into the inner city harvest, even persons who cared little about it in the past. May Christ's love compel many to begin effective inner city evangelism by proclaiming the true Gospel of Jesus Christ with real mercy.

Michael V. Fariss

Step 1

Expanding Your Strategic Planning

In that hour Jesus rejoiced in spirit, and said, "I thank Thee, O Father, Lord of heaven and earth, that Thou hast hid these things from the wise and prudent, and hast revealed them to babes: even so, Father; for it seemed good in Thy sight.
Luke 10:21

1 | Expanding Your Core Values

After these things the Lord appointed other seventy also, and sent them two and two before His face into every city and place, whither He Himself would come. Therefore said He to them, "The harvest is great, but the laborers are few: pray ye therefore the Lord of the harvest, that He would send forth laborers into His harvest." Luke 10:1,2

Jesus is Lord of the **inner city**[1] **spiritual harvest**[2] and we trust Him to make it happen. To begin effective inner city ministry, this conviction must govern a church's, ministry's or individual's mission and vision statements. In the face of dangerous **environments** and overwhelming needs, expanding the breadth of your **strategic planning** to include outreach to impoverished families starts with the **core values** that shape existing ministries.

Leadership's Responsibilities

An organization's core values, though shared by the majority of members, come down from its top leadership.[3] Therefore, leaders of churches, Christian schools, and families determine whether **believers mobilize** for the inner city harvest.

Whether leaders support or undermine this mobilization depends on how well they embrace this harvest as a core value. Transforming leaders' core values to include the inner city spiritual harvest will require them to broaden their belief **paradigms** with moral courage. They must take responsibility for resetting the directions of their ministries and devote time, finances and energy to connect with the inner city.

This is a formidable challenge, since core values are by definition enduring and consistent over time. Strategic planners usually limit their processes to documenting existing core values of organizations rather than changing them or creating new ones, both of which I call for in this book.

Since leaders will give an account to Christ for how they influence the beliefs of their members, they must accept responsibility for determining whether concern for the salvation of their neighboring inner city families is indeed a core value assigned to them by Jesus Christ. If so, they must embrace this value in their own hearts and drive it home among their congregations so that individual laborers will respond to the Lord's call to serve in His inner city harvest.

If evangelical leaders have neglected a core value from Christ, then changing their **philosophies of outreach** must come with contrition, **repentance** and reform. This transformation must become, in obedience to Jesus, a cause that they never give up on even under seemingly impossible circumstances.

Church and Christian school boards should ask the following questions about their values and the inner city harvest:

Do I care about inner city families? Leaders should evaluate their mission statements to determine the answer. The level of their concern for the salvation of inner city families becomes evident in their philosophies of ministry.

If leaders care, then their core value, mission and vision statements should reflect their compassion. Leaders might want to introspectively review their ministries' mission and vision statements before the Lord in anticipation that they might some-day face this question at the Judgment Seat of Christ.

Do I value those in my ministry who care? Churches and schools should commit to empowering laborers for the inner city harvest. When members appeal for more involvement in the inner city, I encourage leaders to enter into prayerful strate-gic planning to determine what gifted people God is providing them to equip their churches or schools for this purpose.

Since leaders set core values for their ministries, they should prepare for the possibility that the Lord has sent caring people into their congregations to edify from the top down. To ensure success, this mobilization should start with leaders taking the first initiatives. They should cast a vision of inner city min-istry for their members and demonstrate ownership of new val-ues by their personal involvement and how they allocate resources.

Leaders should seek to empower such concerned per-sons or risk losing them. Letting them develop isolated pro-grams that do not strategically impact their church's values and mission prevents mobilization of needed laborers. Frustration with existing structures usually turns them towards other evan-gelism opportunities outside of their home churches. I encour-age leaders to cordially value having believers who care about inner city families in their ministries. Leaders should empower them to edify and to mobilize their members for Christ's inner city harvest.

Do I value the role of evangelists? Christ gives evangelists to His Church to prepare His people to carry out the work of evangelism. Since evangelistic fervor must become woven into every fabric of church body life, pastors and church boards should appreciate the importance of including evangelists in their strategic planning. Churches should make giftedness the most importance criteria for choosing evangelistic leadership and enlist persons whom God uses to lead unbelievers to Christ.

Prompted by the Holy Spirit's grace in their lives, these persons already value the spiritual harvest. Because of their giftedness, they pray for more laborers and value equipping them for evangelism.

Some evangelists are gifted for preaching the Gospel from the pulpit, while others are more fruitful in personal, relationship evangelism.[4] Philip's gift, as the evangelist in the book of Acts, was manifested in both personal and mass evangelism.

My colleague, Ken Watson, and I have contrasting kinds of evangelism ministries. Thousands have responded to his evangelistic messages, but he seldom brings persons to Christ through one-on-one witnessing. In comparison, the Lord has blessed my personal evangelism focusing on relationships, but I have seen few come to Christ through preaching. Church leaders should value both kinds of gifted evangelists and encourage their equipping roles.

Personal Values

The personal core values of individuals serving in the inner city harvest must include totally trusting His intervention, protection, sustenance, focus and results much the same as missionaries in foreign countries who depend on God for every aspect of their ministries.

<u>*Value Trusting Jesus Christ for Intervention.*</u> To bolster our faith and values, Luke 10 proclaims Jesus as Lord of the Harvest and reminds us of our privilege to serve as His laborers, even in difficult circumstances. In verse one Jesus appointed seventy persons for a short-term two-by-two evangelistic mission to every town and place that He "was about to go" (NIV).

Jesus knew whom He wanted to send and only Jesus foreknew all the places where He would visit. While making this sending process happen, Jesus reinforces the truth in verse two that He alone rules the harvest and that we must continue to pray that He thrust out laborers.

Jesus demonstrates in Luke 10:1-23 that He chooses to make the harvest happen though us. As the Lord of the Harvest, Jesus selects, thrusts out, relocates, risks, focuses, leads, directs. He also houses, feeds, saves, judges, observes, authorizes, protects, empowers, teaches and rejoices as His sent ones go out for Him. Surely we should highly value serving as His workers, especially in our neighboring inner city communities.

Components of Jesus' commission from verses three and four must also govern our thinking and values regarding mobilizing workers for the inner city harvest: "Go your ways: behold, I send you forth as lambs among wolves. Carry neither purse, nor script, nor shoes; and salute no man by the way." He indicates through these commands our privilege to value and trust His ability to intervene.

A Testimony of How God Works

I rejoice when reflecting on how God intervened in Shaq (a.k.a. Edward) and Terrell's lives. They put their faith in Christ (on the same night) at my dining room table. A few months before when I met this couple they seemed anything but ready for a spiritual harvest in their public housing neighborhood.

Shaq lived in immorality with Terrell even though he was not on her apartment lease. I met him through my **Amateur Athletic Union** (AAU) basketball team because I coached Terrell's daughter, Jasmine. Shaq attended my practices but looked like a troublemaker. I remember praying that particular season, "Lord, why do you send me all the hard cases?"

He seemed years from surrendering to Christ and closely monitored my every move during Jasmine's basketball training. Once when he informed Terrell of my plans to visit them and share the Gospel, she told him, "You had better not bring that white man into my house!"

My first opportunity to spend time with them occurred as we rode two hours to Richmond, Virginia, to appeal on Jasmine's behalf to the AAU State Board. During our state championship game, the frustrated center from the opposing team jumped on Jasmine's back and tried to tackle her. Jasmine instinctively bent down, flipped the attacker over her back, and threw two lightning-quick punches that she had honed during a rough childhood of many inner city fights.

The unsaved lifestyles of these parents, their complicated backgrounds, the new hardships that repentance might create for them and Jasmine's toughness made the task of leading them to Christ seem like an impossible mission.

I admit that facing challenges like these in inner city evangelism significantly conflict with my temperament. Having a Type A personality, I usually intend on making things happen in my world. Although I hear that church planters need self-initiative traits to help them break new ground, the more advanced my evangelism becomes in the inner city, the more I find myself in a state of personal helplessness. Like with Shaq and Terrell, many of my daily prayers now conclude that the only resource that I bring to make things happen is the name of Jesus Christ.

This reality grows as I mobilize workers for this harvest. Strategies that might be sustainable in the suburbs with middle-class families repeatedly loom as impossible, unaffordable, undesirable or dangerous ideas when applied in the inner city. By mobilizing workers for urban evangelism, I find myself encouraging a growing number of believers to adopt the same mindset of personal helplessness and a great sense of dependency upon Christ.

The Lord faithfully opened a door for the Gospel with Jasmine and her family. I had observed Jasmine's extraordinary athletic ability for one practice when she joined my AAU team as a nine-year-old and I knew right away that with her the Lord had given me another opportunity to compete at the national level. In Jasmine's exceptional athletic ability, I saw the potential for our team to win local and state tournaments and qualify for the AAU National Championship.

My initial impressions of Jasmine's basketball talent were correct. She played the toughest brand of basketball that I have ever seen in a young girl. From the beginning, Jasmine competed fiercely. Her emotional leadership and her drive to succeed inspired her teammates to win five consecutive AAU State Championships starting in 1999, which qualified them for the national tournament each year. Yet all the electrifying experiences she gave me on the court pale in comparison to the joy I experienced when I explained to her the good news of Jesus Christ and she accepted Him.

In between the early games at the same State tournament, Shaq sat next to me in the bleachers. He asked, "How do you get your team to play like that – they play in a flow?" He meant that they complimented each other so much during games that they appeared to glide smoothly up and down the basketball court in harmony.

I responded, "It's all Jesus, Shaq. I dedicate this to Jesus and He is the One who makes it work." I had to leave him to begin coaching the girls but my wife Kim continued the conversation. As I watched them talking about the Lord, I knew God's grace was working on Him.

A few weeks later, I purposed to spend three hours a week with Shaq in relationship evangelism. I attended the "Hoop It Up" outdoor basketball three-on-three tournament on one Saturday because I knew he would be there all day. When rain delayed the games, we found a McDonalds and waited out the bad weather. Our conversation about spiritual issues went so well I asked if I could come to his apartment and talk about the Lord with Terrell and him. He hesitated, but eventually agreed to let me come over. We set the meeting for the following Monday because Terrell worked on Sundays. Thankfully, God's grace was at work in Terrell's life as well.

I arrived at their public housing neighborhood that Monday evening not knowing what to expect. I carefully parked on the narrow street that circled next to Terrell's apartment to prevent offending any of the other residents. Shaq let me into the living room and we sat on the sofa while we waited for Terrell to arrive. When she came home, she sat on the carpet next to this sofa. I asked her how things were going and she immediately burst into tears. She explained how her boss had just fired her the day before.

God used this hurt and conflicts within her family to break down her resistance to meeting with me. Over the next month Kim and I met several times to study the Bible with them.

Each time they stopped short of turning to Christ because of they did not think they could survive without living together in immorality. They expressed desires to get married but feared that getting married would result in their eviction from the public housing neighborhood because Shaq had been living there without permission.

Terrell had already suffered homelessness as a young mother and knew from experience the seriousness of this dilemma. She was fourteen years old when she became pregnant with Jasmine. Now she had another child and also cared for two nieces, so the prospect of risking homelessness by committing to Jesus Christ filled her with fear.

In spite of this, the Lord kept drawing them to Himself. They returned to our home every week to study the Bible. One evening they arrived noticeably upset. That morning they had awakened to find a pile of burned clothing near an electrical outlet in their children's bedroom. They explained how Jasmine, who usually slept through any noise, heard the smoke alarm in the middle of the night. She got out of bed, put out the fire and then went back to sleep. The cinderblock walls and concrete ceilings probably prevented Shaq and Terrell from hearing the alarm. Nothing prevented them from recognizing this wake-up call from God.

I reminded Shaq and Terrell that unless they put their faith in Jesus Christ, they faced consequences worse than homelessness and an earthly fire. By continually rejecting Jesus' wonderful offer of salvation, they put themselves and their children in danger of God's eternal punishment in the Lake of Fire. I challenged them to repent and trust in Jesus Christ. I said, "If you obey Jesus Christ and get 'put out' of your apartment, then you can stand on the street with your belongings, look up to heaven and say, 'Lord Jesus, I believe in You!'"

Shaq and Terrell surrendered to Jesus Christ that evening! I knew that their decision was genuine when Shaq moved out of Terrell's apartment and lived with his mother until their wedding day.

They braced themselves for the possibility of eviction as they prepared to inform the Housing Authority of their marriage. I offered to call the Housing Authority to intercede for them and they accepted my offer. As the phone rang during my call to their apartment manager, I prayed. When I heard a voice on the other end of the line, I introduced myself. Before I could go on the manager interjected, "Mike, it has been a long time. How are you doing?"

The Lord gave us instant favor with this man whose daughter had been in my **Fellowship of Christian Athletes** club almost twenty years earlier. The manager worked with Shaq and Terrell and enabled them to remain. They eventually moved into an apartment outside of the public housing complex. I turned the team over to him to be their head coach.

One Sunday afternoon, I took my daughter, Joanna, who was ten at the time, and her Christian teammate, Kelsey, to visit Jasmine. We purposed to share the Gospel with her, but my young partners seemed skeptical about the prospect of Jasmine even listening to us, since she lacked any kind of spiritual background. Shaq and Terrell busied themselves in the kitchen while Joanna, Kelsey and I talked with Jasmine in the living room of their public housing apartment.

As I explained salvation and emphasized how Jesus had died on the cross to pay the punishment for her sins, Jasmine put both hands over her face and began weeping. For twenty minutes she sobbed silently in this position with tears running down her forearms. When Shaq checked on us he gave me a questioning look, but turned around and went back to the kitchen while I continued explaining the Gospel.

Eventually, Jasmine composed herself and gave her life to Christ. I praise God for including me in this family's harvest in the hood. Multiply the joy and praise from this report many times over to understand why I consider myself quite blessed in God's economy.

Value the Privilege of Trusting Christ for Protection. The Lord watches over His laborers as He sends them into dangerous circumstances "like lambs in the midst of wolves." He commissions them to follow in His footsteps and thereby endure the threats of Satan, his forces of darkness, and the evil people under their control. We overcome them by the blood of the Lamb and the word of our testimony, not by shrinking from danger (Rev. 12:11).

Entering the harvest to face dangers associated with the inner city runs opposite to the movement of today's evangelical families towards the suburbs of the "Red States." Taking their calling as parents seriously, they sacrificially invest in their families and avoid dangerous environments to protect their children.[5] Fear remains a deterrent to mobilizing workers for the inner city, even when the suburbs present many risks as well. Over a third of white evangelicals put moral values first among their domestic concerns compared to 16 percent of African-Americans Christians.[6] Sociologists Michael Emerson and Christian Smith conclude that the majority of evangelical laity in America believe that their churches should provide comfort in a troubled world. These Christians are consumers rather than producers of love and concern and they resent attempts by church leaders to change the status quo.[7]

Evangelicals must value and make a decision to trust the Lord to protect them and their families if they are to join the inner city harvest. I have a son and three daughters who are between the ages of 21 and 13 at the time of writing this book. When I question the wisdom of exposing my children to dangerous inner city places and their negative influences, remembering one particular small scare reinforces my conviction to trust in God, and not in the suburbs, to protect them.

When our first child, Rebekah, was two years old, she fell into a suburban swimming pool. Just when I sensed the need to cross the pool to spend time with her, I saw her fall in. I came to her as she thrashed her arms and legs but stayed about a foot below the surface. Looking frantically up through the clear water, she remained unnoticed by those playing around her. I scooped her up into my arms, thanking the Lord for protecting her in the suburbs. Although I am careful in the inner city, my ultimate trust is in the Lord.

The protection of the Lord is also available to families who dare to penetrate society's darkness rather than fleeing it to evade its negative influences. The children of families who follow the Lord of the Harvest into potentially dangerous environments receive the ultimate reward of discovering the intervening power of His Gospel and protection. They also have opportunities to learn how to live courageously among different lifestyles while preserving Christian family values. They may practice becoming "salt and light" in their communities under the guidance of their parents and the protection of their Lord.

When fears prevent evangelicals from mobilizing into the inner city, they also expose a lack of faith and love for Christ who controls the harvest. Passing on these fears to our children may prevent their obedience to His commission by teaching them to deny Him to avoid potentially dangerous environments.

Someone has said that a measure of a man is what it takes to stop him. We must repent of lifestyles shaped by fears, and instead follow our unstoppable Lord into His harvest field, trusting Him to protect.

Best of all, children ministering with their parents in the inner city harvest grow up understanding from experience Christ's commission to cross racism's divides. For example, during Christmas times when my children were young, our ministry team recreated live manger scenes in inner city neighborhoods to share the Gospel. Each year we recruited volunteers to build a stable and we rented animals that attracted visitors.

Our staff team and families dressed in biblical costumes, presented a Christmas skit and played music in downtown communities. After we set up the nativity scene, volunteers from churches caroled throughout the neighborhood handing out gospel pamphlets and inviting families to come.

I considered the hard work of providing these evangelistic events as a gift to Christ from our ministry team's families. In return, these outreaches made wonderful and lasting impressions on our children.

On one particular cold December night I watched as my daughter Joanna, only four years old at the time, interacted with a girl her age in a public housing neighborhood. This girl, whom we had just met, volunteered to play the role of Mary in our nativity scene. She used her black doll baby to represent Jesus, since we had always asked a girl from each neighborhood to provide the baby for the manger. Joanna, dressed as a shepherd and holding her own doll, joined her at the straw-filled manger.

Both girls sat silently together while adults sang carols

and preached to passerbys on the street. Then this black child looked compassionately upon Joanna's unprotected white baby doll. Without speaking, she stood and gently took my daughter's doll from her arms and carefully tucked it into the "swaddling clothes" that covered her baby doll Jesus.

We conducted our Christmas outreach with two dolls in the manger, a black baby and a white baby, wrapped together! Our families experienced Christmas's wonderful reconciliation during these nights of ministry with inner city children and parents in their neighborhoods.

Sometimes our children received valuable lessons at "the school of hard knocks" that equipped them to communicate and relate well cross-culturally. At age seven, my son, Brent, played for an inner city soccer club. A black Moslem directed this club, black parents from Moslem and Christian backgrounds coached the teams and Brent was the only white participant.

I came home from work one day and Kim informed me that Brent had been in a fight with an older black friend who lived nearby. When I confronted Brent, he declared emphatically that he did not fight but that the other boy had hit him for no reason. I asked if he had said anything mean to provoke the other child but he insisted that he had not. Brent recalled saying something before getting hit, which is now commonly known as the N-word.

Obviously he did not understand the seriousness of using this word so I entered into a lecture on its horrible history. Then I told him that some black parents tell their children to punch white persons who call them that name. Brent said, "That's not fair. The kids on my soccer team call me that all the time."

Sure enough, during the next soccer match as Brent skillfully dodged defenders, an excited black dad shouted out, "That nigger can play!" Brent learned from this experience how to choose his phrases wisely because some words offend African-Americans when they come from the lips of white people.

Although a knee injury ended his high school soccer career, lessons on cultural sensitivity like this one in the inner city prepared him to maneuver well through racial divides.

Jesus' ultimate control over the entire assignment that He gave his disciples in Luke 10 becomes evident when He tells them in verse 18 that He had watched their spiritual victory as "Satan fell like lightning from heaven." During their witness, Jesus provides them spiritual protection through His authoritative name by making demons, snakes and scorpions submit to them. Christ still protects His sent ones today and gives them the spiritual authority to "overcome all the power of the enemy" (Luke 10:19,20).

Praise Jesus Christ who keeps His promise to always remain with us as His Spirit empowers our witness. It is our privilege to depend on Him, even when we feel helpless in the inner city harvest.

Value the Privilege of Trusting Christ for Sustenance. As Lord of the harvest, Jesus also asks His followers to make personal sacrifices. He told the seventy-two workers sent out in Luke 10:4 to trust Him for their daily needs and not to bring with them a purse, bag or sandals. Although Scripture does not give the length of their assignment, comparing the first four books of the New Testament indicates that their outreach project could have lasted several months. Jesus demonstrated that He takes responsibility for the financial needs of His laborers as He makes the harvest happen.

Since inner city work targets impoverished families, the

opportunity exists for His evangelists to serve in an ocean of need. For example, my wife, Kim, and I currently mentor a young girl named Sharquitta Brown, whom we enrolled in educational therapy to overcome a learning disability. She lives where poverty, drugs, prostitution and violence prevail.

I met her when she was seven years old as she smiled and ran beside my van in this challenging neighborhood. Often when I came to drop off her sister at their home after AAU basketball games, I would see Sharquitta playing in the narrow one-way streets that ran a few yards from her front door. I promised the Lord that I would help her if He would make a way possible.

Since then, as the Father to the fatherless, the Lord has faithfully opened amazing doors to assist Sharquitta through our church, sports and educational outreaches. After she had been held back in the second grade for two years in a row, we enrolled her in an facility called the **Park Place School** where she first received **educational therapy**. Now she receives financial aid and support from individuals to attend a Christian school where she continues this one-on-one therapy. She also attends with our family and participates in our camping ministries.

After our ministry team conducted a summer Bible club for about twenty children on her block in 2004, she invited her best friend to attend church with us. On the way I asked the friend about her grades in school. The friend told me that she had remained in the third grade even though she was eleven years old, but her mother for some reason had just had her skipped to the fifth grade. I felt overwhelmed as I realized that the friend's educational needs exceeded Sharquitta's problems. Looking around, I prayed for the many other needy children playing on their block.

Like the learning disability therapy at the Park Place

School, effective inner city evangelistic ministries often become expensive and financially less attractive to donors. High cost-per-person ratios discourage support of these kinds of interventions, despite their tremendous positive impact .

Even when an outreach proves affordable, the vastness of the need and the harvest in the inner city should motivate us to replicate effective ministries even when they seem beyond available resources in the natural. Praise Jesus Christ that He is responsible for funding them.

I believe that our greatest asset for inner city ministry comes from the poor themselves. Our Lord gave His word to respond to widows or orphans when He said, "If . . . they do cry out to Me, I will surely hear their cry . . . for I am compassionate" (Exodus 22:23, 27 NIV). I find children crying out to God as they suffer in conditions of poverty. I ask God to remember His promises to deliver them and to graciously empower me to extend mercy and justice. The prayers of desperate children may literally be calling down heaven to thrust out laborers into their neighborhoods.

We also possess this kind of leverage in our prayers. We can never show more mercy than Christ. If the Lord obligated Himself to fatherless children, then He must respond to our cries for mercy on their behalf.

I admit that I do not know why the prayers of many children went unheeded through slavery and the injustices of the Jim Crow era. May their blood still cry out and join the prayers rising from our inner cities today to move the stewards of God's resources to finance the Lord's harvest.

Past the seeker as he prayed came the crippled and the beggar and the beaten. And seeing them

. . .he cried, "Great God, how is it that a loving creator can see such things and yet do nothing about them?" God said, "I did do something. I made you."
Author Unknown[8]

Value Making the Lord's Inner City Harvest One's Focus.
The commands Jesus gave His seventy evangelists in Luke 10:4 included requiring them to remain focused on their mission to the extent of even avoiding interruptions by not greeting persons on the road! Jesus still makes His Great Commission our focus today because He came "to seek and to save that which was lost."

I have noticed how easily believers in the U.S. can be distracted by T.V., video games, the internet, sports, committees, the stock market and a seemingly unending list of activities, all of which may promote earthly, temporal values. For example, in our relational evangelism training, we ask each participant to dedicate three hours a week to spending quality time with unbelievers. Even with high accountability, distractions make budgeting three hours, out of 168 per week, a difficult challenge for most persons!

We also encourage new inner city believers to avoid chasing previously unaffordable distractions when their lives stabilize. Jesus calls His sent ones to a strategy of "distraction prevention." As our heavenly Father seeks to make us more fruitful for the inner city harvest, it is our privilege to remove distractions that cause us to lose focus on our mission.

Value the Privilege of Trusting Jesus for the Results. In Luke 10:5, we also observe Jesus introducing the "man of peace" strategy: "When you enter a house, first say, 'Peace to this house.' If a man of peace is there, your peace will rest on him." Jesus goes on to provide specific details for a short-term plan for that time and place, which include several transferable principles that I will discuss in Step Four. His grace and mercy provide peace that opens hearts for the Gospel.

Jesus explains in Luke 10:16 that He determines and measures the results of this plan. He takes personally the rejection of His ambassadors by unbelievers. "He who listens to you listens to Me; he who rejects you rejects Me; but he who rejects Me rejects Him who sent Me." Fortunately, His sent ones do not have to concern themselves with the condemning process. The Lord of the Harvest takes care of judging the lost - even entire cities (verses 13-15).

When evaluating results, evangelicals ministering to the poor should value first of all the growth in their own lives. Catholic missionaries make a good point when saying, "The poor will evangelize you." The poor edify through their patient endurance in adversity without bitterness. They teach simplicity, creativity, prayerful dependence on God and how to be transparent.[9] The Lord of the Harvest inspires and matures His laborers with these lessons.

A recent response to the Gospel illustrates how serving in the inner city blesses me. While waiting with my basketball team for an evening game, I sat on a gym's shiny floor and leaned against its closed wooden bleachers. A girl from the track team, who had been attending our Fellowship of Christian Athlete meetings, came and sat next me.

I offered to help her prepare for her exams so she opened her book bag and she began reviewing a social studies handout. She impressed me as a young person whose strong study habits will make a way out of the poverty she experiences in her public housing environment. Despite her family's background, her diligence in the classroom and vibrant personality reveal her amazing resiliency and determination.

When I noticed that her study guide covered church history, I asked her about John Calvin and what he thought about getting into heaven. She replied, "He believed that God elected some for heaven and elected others for damnation." Her answer provided me an opportunity to explain the Gospel of Jesus Christ.

When I finished, this girl sat silently for a few seconds and then asked, "Coach Mike, when they say at FCA that you should open your heart to Christ, what do they mean?" She told me that she had never taken this step.

While I calmly spoke about God's gift of salvation, tears streamed down her face faster than she could wipe them away. I suggested that she verbalize her faith in Christ in a prayer, because these tears convinced me that the Holy Spirit had convicted her heart to receive Him. Although theologians, since Calvin's day, debate how salvation occurs, I am grateful that I was there when conversion happened in this remarkable young person. Through this girl's sincere response, I found my own heart opening wider to Jesus and His wonderful spiritual harvest.

Ministry Values

Inner city ministries should be launched with the following specific core values guiding their strategic objectives:

1. Extending mercy and justice are priorities when fulfill ing the purposes of God.
2. Inner city ministry must be based on relationships in

the community where evangelism and discipleship reach entire families in their homes.

3. Local churches strategies must target inner city men.
4. Local churches must equip and mobilize inner city residents to fulfill the Great Commission in their neighborhoods and and around the world.

Core Value Inventory

1. Copy this table and write out your personal, ministry and school's mission statements:

My Personal Mission	My Ministry's Mission	My School's Mission

2. What components of these mission statements reflect concern for inner city families?

3. How do these mission statements indicate neglect of the inner city harvest?

4. Check the core values that shape your ministry's vision. Put an X next to the core values that you anticipate will become difficult for your ministry to embrace.

__ We care about inner city families and value their salvation.

__ We elevate the role of evangelists in shaping strategic planning.

__ We trust in Jesus' intervention in the lives of inner city families.

__ We value opportunities to trust Jesus' protection.

__ We value trusting Jesus for sustenance.

__ We value making the spiritual harvest our life's focus.

__ We trust Jesus for the results of the spiritual harvest.

__ We promote mercy and justice as priorities in God's purposes.

__ We value evangelism that is based on community relationships

__ We value inner city men and target them for evangelism.

__ We value empowering inner city believers to fulfill Christ's Great Commission at home and abroad.

5. Action Steps: Dedicate a page in your prayer journal to record requests and pray for the inner city every day. Ask the Lord to send laborers into specific neighborhoods. List the names of your ministry leaders and ask God to strategically guide them regarding the inner city.

2 | Expanding Your Mission

"... rejoice, because your names are written in heaven."
Luke 10:20

Before effectively mobilizing workers for the inner city, evangelical leaders must first clear the major huddle of including the inner city poor in the **missions** of their lives and ministries. This requires courageously expanding the reasons why their ministries exist, the types of people they target, and the kinds of ministries they produce.[1] They must lead their families, churches and schools in putting Christ's inner city harvest into their hearts and missions regardless of whether they are located in (or near) impoverished urban communities.

Evangelicals must begin to think strategically enough to believe that their lives, families, churches and schools exist for certain purposes, which *include* evangelizing impoverished, inner city families. As explained in Chapter 1, for most evangelicals this kind of thinking requires reforming their personal, church and school's core values.

From childhood, my daughter Rebekah had a clear perspective of this challenge because growing up in two worlds gave her a unique point of view. In one world, she attended a Christian elementary school and fellowshipped with our family's friends and partnering suburban churches.

At the same time she lived out our family's inner city

church planting experiences and inherited our beliefs concerning the need to reach out to the inner city poor. Rebekah played basketball and attended camp with urban children during the dangerous drug crisis after crack first became prevalent on Norfolk's streets the late 1980's. Also, with our other children, she worshiped with inner city families in a low-income, government subsidized apartment complex and participated in our youth ministries there. The main spiritual difference between her suburban world with evangelical churches and schools, and our family's inner city world became evident to her through their contrasting missions. Her suburban classmates and friends did not include evangelizing inner city families in their purposes for existing, the type of people they targeted or the kind of ministries they produced.

As an elementary school student, Rebekah revealed that she recognized the differences between her two worlds when she made a simple but strategic observation one day about mobilizing workers for the inner city harvest. We happened to drive through a large inner city community that she did not recognize. As we passed block after inner city block, Rebekah become conscious of its vast size and many kinds of needs.

Since she valued evangelism, she concluded that I should go there and bring change through the same kind of ministry we provided in a neighboring community called Huntersville. She also understood my reasoning when I responded that I could not work in another community because our present ministry responsibilities swamped us.

After a few seconds of strategic thinking, Rebekah challenged me to go to certain large suburban evangelical churches and persuade them to minister like me in this neighborhood. For all the people that attended these churches, compared with the few persons working with us in Huntersville, she surmised that they should have enough manpower for the task.

She became excited about her plan and said, "You could ask their pastors to preach to the people and get workers to come here." When I doubted that her idea would work, she reacted, "I thought you said that they were good pastors." Rebekah soon realized that leaders in her two worlds did not have the same sense of mission regarding reaching inner city families for Christ.

Unbridled Optimism

I believe that the time has come to implement Rebekah's plan (doesn't Scripture say, "out of the mouth of babes . . ."), but on a grander scale. As the Lord mobilizes Christians for inner city outreach today, evangelical leaders across our country have unprecedented opportunities to think as strategically about the spiritual harvest in the inner city, considering its eternal results. The following reasons support my optimism about the current window of opportunity for transforming the missions of local churches to include the inner city harvest:

Cultural Shifts. American society's recent cultural shift towards unprecedented acceptance of racial diversity positively impacts the values of believers and provides cultural advantages for expanding the missions of churches to include the inner city.

Today most Christians interrelate with persons of other races and socio-economic backgrounds in their neighborhoods, work places and schools. Many "Echo Boomers," the 80 million young people in the U.S. born in America between 1982 and 1995, expect and even value racial diversity. Racially homogeneous churches stand out as oddities in their present-day culture. Many young evangelicals recognize this problem in their churches and support ending racial division in worship. Like Rebekah, Christians may now believe in unchanging doctrine and still adapt their organizational cultures to cross these race and class divides.

Other changes in present-day society strengthen the cultural shifts. Many older leaders, like Senator Robert Byrd, who once staunchly fought racial integration now express remorse over their previous racist platforms. Senior Christians who still support segregation leave their church resources to a generation that as a whole values racial reconciliation.

Since 9/11, U.S. citizens have generously helped disaster victims indicating a stronger culture of caring for persons in crisis. Many opened their homes to families displaced by the devastation from the hurricane in 2005 named Katrina. Even the United States military expanded its mission in Afghanistan and Iraq beyond killing enemies to sacrificially providing humanitarian assistance to win the hearts of people and the war against terrorism. This growing compassion and strategically expanding missions give me hope that God's people will also purposefully respond to the plight of inner city families.

Growing Influences of Compassionate Christians. I have observed an increasing number of Christians connecting with inner city families and becoming committed to helping the poor in all areas and to mercy ministry. From the beginning of my urban work in 1980, I have come across persons in churches who have a deep conviction about ministry to the poor and long to see their churches involved in inner city ministry. Although often frustrated, most have faithfully waited on the Lord for change in their churches' missions. Some have provided my base of financial and prayer support over the years. Because the Lord is raising up more and more persons committed to inner city ministry, the time has come to raise our voices and call entire congregations to action!

The urban ministry landscape is changing for the good as God is burdening these persons of influence to care about inner city families. When I began urban ministry in 1980, the idea of a white person working in the inner city seemed inconceivable to many black and white Christians who discouraged it.

Now, inner city ministry has become like an industry that recruits whites, and persons of every race, for missions trips, internships and short or long-term assignments. I also hear from church members who independently develop relationships with persons from the inner city and then call me for advice on how to effectively help them.

My optimism increases as I come across more evangelists and persons in the body of Christ with the gift of mercy striving to find ways to involve their congregations in the inner city. Often frustrated by institutionalized barriers that promote racial division, many such persons resort to fulfilling their ministries through parachurch outreaches or raise their support and go to the foreign mission field. The time has come for leaders to empower these gifted ones to equip others in their churches for the work of evangelism.

Changed Hearts. If the Lord is powerful enough to transform a lost drug addict's mind, as I have witnessed several times, then He also can turn the hearts of His people towards the inner city harvest. He is in the business of creating change. I want to stay *ahead of the curve* as God's grace revives His people to fulfill Christ's commission in the inner city with those who are **poverty** stricken.

God must transform the missions of churches and not just their mission statements. The conviction to serve in the inner city must come from changed hearts and not just new documents. Churches must implement strategic plans that revamp their mission statements and not let them sit in their files and make little difference. So I appeal to church leaders: open your hearts to God's changing power and embrace your inner city neighbors in your church missions.

The book of Nehemiah provides principles for preparing hearts for action. Nehemiah, whom God used to provide the vision and leadership to rebuild the walls of Jerusalem, spent months in prayer about this need as he repented for his nation's sin. When the Lord provided him the opportunity to act on his prayers, Nehemiah entered into strategic planning, called on the remnant of God's people to rise and build, and led the way in spite of opposition.

Church leaders from different congregations in our metropolitan area of Hampton Roads, Virginia, have been praying for fifteen years for the salvation of our inner city residents and for reconciliation between the races. As God is turning Christian's hearts towards this cause, these leaders should strategically plan like this Old Testament leader did so well.

Strategic Leadership. I may be going out on a limb to say that today's Christian leaders are becoming more aware of the benefits of strategic planning to their ministries. The process of prayerfully organizing to accomplish strategic objectives also opens many new and often unexpected opportunities to begin serving the poor. When implemented with accountability, strategic plans keenly break through **structural barriers** that prevent the mobilization of Christians seeking to make a lasting difference in ministry.

Effective strategic planning brings about needed paradigm shifts when ministries' organizational cultures become more flexible and adaptable to change. This kind of transformation in ministries comes about when leaders encourage departure from tradition, practice strategic decision making and empower change-oriented members to implement mechanisms that bring action.[2] When leaders prepare their ministries to support change for strategic planning purposes, they take the take the first step towards ending divides that undermine the inner city harvest.

Demise of Churches. Like the sobering reality of watching families commit their loved ones to the grave, the demise of churches is awakening God's people to the fact that congregations of all races must obediently love their neighbors or die. Several white churches in Norfolk face extinction because they did not welcome the black families who moved into their surrounding neighborhoods. These churches did not adapt when the racial and socio-economic demographics of their communities changed. Commuting in and out from the suburbs to attend church they have yet to join the inner city harvest even though their neighborhoods became home to impoverished families decades ago. Although **gentrification** may give them new hope that white middle class families will once again attend their beautiful buildings, their present crisis cautions other churches to open their hearts and doors to their diverse neighbors.

Faith in the Lord of the Harvest. I believe in Jesus Christ and in His power to thrust out His people into the inner city by whatever means necessary. For this reason, I am confident in the potential for mobilizing churches for the inner city harvest when God arises and calls His people into service. Let us all faithfully pray, "Lord of the Harvest, thrust out your laborers into the inner city. Turn every church inside-out to serve inner city families for Christ's sake!"

Mission Theology

Jesus, in Luke 10:20, helps us strip away all the confusion over the personal and corporate values that influence the **mission statements** of our ministries. Although He had empowered them to defeat Satan and the forces of darkness, in this Scripture Jesus instructed His disciples to rejoice that their names are written in the **Book of Life**. With this one sentence He turns the perspectives of His **evangelists** toward heaven.

By directing His disciples to rejoice in their present status in heaven, He set a target for planning our mission statements ". . . on things which are above where Christ sitteth on the right hand of God" (Col. 3:1). By finding happiness in the present through the glory of heaven, Jesus gives Christians the following eternal reasons for including inner city families in their missions.

Eternal Gratitude Elevates Our Aims. Luke 10:20 reminds us that the value of the unmerited glory received in our own, individual salvation far outweighs any of our life achievements. Jesus' gracious eternal work of including us in His spiritual harvest deserves such gratitude that eternity with Christ becomes our source of joy, even beyond the excitement of exercising spiritual power.

What Jesus did for us infinitely exceeds in value anything and everything that we will ever do for Him. In the most hopeless situations, God's sent ones should remain eternal optimists.

Though spiritual warfare becomes intense in evangelism, we can endure the worst by keeping in mind our present eternal relationship with Christ.

Focusing on Him with this eternal perspective, we no longer need demonstrations of spiritual power to give us confidence. With nothing to lose and nothing to prove, we may become content with godliness, bold in the face of rejection, generous while in poverty and secure in our self-worth. We walk by faith when we make our Lord's gift of eternal life our sustaining, unwavering source of joy.

In addition, the more we value this eternal status with Christ, the more other ambitions melt away so we may think strategically and reform our mission statements. To grasp our present standing in heaven, believers in our Lord should imagine being there, glancing down at our names written in the Book of Life and then looking up into the face of Jesus.

Created for this relationship with Him, this position in heaven epitomizes why we exist. What else matters when we face Christ? Values related to programs, possessions, buildings, wealth, security, recognition, race, status and power evaporate. Our only concern in the present, as we rejoice in Jesus, is about others and whether their names are also written in heaven.

Accountability in Eternity Shapes Our Objectives. As heirs of eternal life, we accept with enormous gratitude and sense of indebtedness the serious responsibility of fulfilling the mission entrusted to us by Jesus Christ in Matthew 28:18-20: ". . . Go and make disciples of all nations . . ." (Matt. 28:19 NIV). We become stewards of Jesus' Gospel and look forward to giving an account in His presence for the eternal impact we had made on others' lives in our brief lifetimes. Rejoicing in our relationship with Christ, we should aim to fulfill His mission.

Those serving as Christian leaders have the privilege and expectation of higher accountability before Christ in eternity. Leaders, gratefully setting their values on eternal life with Christ, accept responsibility for equipping their members to obey the mission statement that He gave. Obedience to this mission makes our lives eternally significant.

Christ's Commission Includes the Inner City. To fulfill Jesus' mandate, leaders must also assume responsibility for including the evangelization of neighboring inner city families in their ambitions, objectives, goals and budgeting. Although broadening the missions and visions of local churches and Christian schools to value serving inner city families may seem like formidable structural leaps of faith, leaders of these ministries should envision someday having to give an account to the Lord about whether they included impoverished neighbors in their strategic plans, schedules and budgets.

A Generation of African-Americans Grapple With Eternity's Significance. The following sections in this book explain why strategically expanding mission statements to include the inner city harvest is a vital work of repentance and reconciliation. In the past, when teaching slaves to submit, white people used the hope of eternal glory as an incentive despite the inherent obvious oppressiveness of slavery.

This evil scheme, which must have come straight from Satan, corrupted the Gospel's hope and joy to them. Satan now uses hurt to obscure the true Gospel by deceiving many African-Americans into believing that heaven is the white man's oppressive **"pie-in-the-sky"** doctrine and that joy will come from their accomplishments or financial successes in this life.

Inner city black young people grow up hearing many challenges about getting a good education, getting out of the ghetto and taking momma with them. I have attended many sports banquets where the speakers repeat the edict that education is the ticket to enjoying the **American Dream**.

Young black people who do succeed educationally often pursue this dream in middle class suburbia. When Jesus asks them to refocus their lives on His spiritual harvest and on eternity, they allow the pull of materialism to keep them from making the sacrifices required to return to minister in the inner city or to serve abroad. As a result, a large majority of the black middle-class still misses out on their destiny to fulfill Christ's Great Commission, and most white Christians do not notice or seem to mind the loss.

I have observed the need for Christians to prayerfully balance making sacrifices for the sake of the Gospel with their physical, emotional and spiritual survival needs. Whether in urban America or on a foreign missions field, wholehearted obedience to the Great Commission often requires laborers to act contrary to basic drives for personal survival.

Usually the more resources a Christian devotes to laboring in the spiritual harvest, the less he or she has to pursue survival in this life. Likewise, the more we reserve resources for survival, the less we can invest in the harvest. Trying to regulate the balance between these two trade-offs in missionary service, sometimes I focus more on surviving than the harvest and other times I expend myself by focusing more on the harvest than on meeting my basic needs.

Eternity is so significant that Jesus often calls His followers to focus on the spiritual harvest at the expense of personal survival in this life. He promised that in this life and in the life to come He would reward sacrifices made for Him. I have experienced many rewarding assignments in this life that I attribute to Christ's promise. By faith we look forward to the eternal glory of Christ that has yet to be revealed to us. For if we suffer with Him, His Word promises that we will also reign with Him.

This creates a new challenge for many middle class African-Americans who as survivors of poverty seem to struggle with giving themselves sacrificially for Christ's commission. They may continue to live with a survivalist mentality even after they become financially secure. I noticed survivalist tendencies in my wife's grandparents who came from Italy and settled in West Virginia. They stored enough supplies in their attic and freezer to endure another Great Depression! Without generational wealth to provide a financial safety net, many in the black middle-class still live like survivalists while pursuing the money to preserve their lifestyles.

Time will tell them that the American Dream "is not all that it is cracked up to be." My wife Kim and I grew up in the same white middle class neighborhood, one of the nicest in Virginia Beach. In 1973, our community epitomized the suburban lifestyle so well that TIME Magazine used our high school to illustrate the growth of American suburbs, capturing a picture of Kim getting on a school bus. Although persons from the inner city might become infatuated with the blessings of our middle class lifestyle, they must consider that families suffer in the suburbs as well.

Consider these examples of how families in my middle-class neighborhood suffered: My sixth grade teacher's son died of muscular dystrophy. The following year, a teenager from my church died in the Vietnam War. A high school classmate died from meningitis. An eleventh grade classmate accidentally ignited an open jar of gasoline with a cigarette, which exploded in his car in front of a suburban shopping mall. He died a few days later. A neighbor's father died in a tractor accident. Five teens and a child from our neighborhood died in separate car accidents over a three year period. A classmate shot his foster parents with a shotgun while they slept. Several friends' parents died of cancer and heart attacks. A friend's father sexually abused him. Several friends grieved over their parents' divorces or agonized through teenage pregnancies. Twenty years after I was in his seventh grade math class, my former teacher committed suicide after murdering his wife and teenage daughter. The environment may be different, but living in the suburbs does not guarantee happiness, a long life or lasting security.

Sorrow winds its way through the suburbs' waterfront communities and country clubs. Suffering does not respect neighborhood boundaries. How many middle class families have worked hard pursuing the American dream only to see their security stolen by suffering and their joy from wealth replaced by bitterness? Working during college at a country club, I saw wealthy men and women drink their retirements away in its clubhouse.

No matter how secure one becomes, age, sickness and death catch up to us all. The words of Jesus provide the solution for those tempted to seek their joy in temporal riches, "But store up for yourselves treasures in heaven ..." (Matt. 6:20 NIV). The words of the psalmist illustrate the tragedy of those who will not listen, "The ransom for a life is costly, no payment is ever enough - that he should live on forever and not see decay. A man who has riches without understanding is like the beasts that perish" (Ps. 49:8,9. . . 20 NIV).

Jesus promised that whoever loses his or her life for His sake will find it, but in the period when slavery existed white oppressors abused this doctrine to manipulate blacks into submission. When forced to lose their lives, blacks resisted this injustice and became survivalists. Though this survival mentality still pervades their culture to some degree, African-Americans who overcome poverty win the freedom to voluntarily lose their lives for Christ and His harvest.

Those who become the first in their families to graduate from certain levels of education may now choose to become the first to sacrifice their security and invest their lives in the inner city or in world missions. Living by faith and getting thrust out by the Lord of the harvest will radically challenge one's values and dreams. Our Heavenly Father performs this transformational work on His sent ones that we might bear fruit having eternal results (John 15:1,2).

African-Americans pursuing the American Dream risk losing the greatest opportunity for black enterprise. Nothing in the American Dream compares with fulfilling Jesus' priceless commission of Matthew 28:18-20! If Maslow's "hierarchy of needs" diagram holds true, self-sacrificial ministry may seem more reasonable to the black middle class's second generation who grow up feeling more secure.

This second generation should eventually want more from life than getting their needs and wants met, while their parents may continue to seek to save their lives. Satan tempts middle class African-Americans to sit out of Christ's harvest. Sadly, those who buy his lies may forfeit present and eternal rewards in their quest for justice and security in this life.

A saying, passed on from mentor to mentor and eventually to me, applies here: "If you succeed without suffering, it is because someone else has suffered before you. If you suffer without succeeding, it is because someone will succeed without suffering after you." African-Americans who have been focusing their lives on financial success may now choose to suffer sacrificially to establish a new kind of spiritual legacy. Proud of their forefathers' enduring struggle through oppression, they may now willingly suffer sacrificial hardships for the sake of families still caught in poverty.

In gratitude for the Lord Jesus' sacrificial intervention in their lives and in obedience to His **Great Commission**, they may humble themselves and take the form of servants as He did. This kind of sacrificial lifestyle will create a legacy of hope for the next generation of inner city young people. In setting aside their rights to enjoy the prosperity of middle class America, they will find and give new life through Jesus Christ's eternal harvest.

The Gospel's Message Is at Stake. Evangelists must also fulfill their responsibilities to equip God's people to proclaim a biblically accurate and clear message about how to receive eternal life. The 2004 elections highlighted several surprising trends about evangelicals that demonstrate the importance of establishing theological convictions about one's need for a spiritual new birth to inherit eternal life.

Some political analysts identify a subset of Christian voters made up of one-third to two-fifths of white evangelicals. These analysts call this subset "freestyle evangelicals" representing 8 to 10 percent of the entire nation's electorate. This group had been considered swing voters and up-for-grabs in the election before most voted Republican to prevent the legalization of gay marriages.

Freestyle evangelicals are more moderate in politics than

the religious right but still hold conservative views on moral values. Their concern for education, health care and the environment comes from their high levels of commitment to protect their children and communities. The majority of freestyle evangelicals are married, live in the suburbs of the Republican voting "Red States" and attend non-denominational churches in the South and West. They hold many traditional beliefs but not as strictly and as fervently as more conservative evangelicals.[3]

Another recent analysis shows a subset of evangelicals who have somehow doctrinally disconnected Christ's spiritual harvest from the right to enter heaven. They are not dogmatic about whether persons need to be born again to receive eternal life. Only half of white evangelicals and 42 percent of black evangelicals say they believe that only born again Christians go to heaven.[4]

I expect that both of these two evangelical subgroups, the political freestylers and those who do not believe in the necessity of being "**born again**" for salvation, include mostly the same people. Apparently, they are not only swing-voting politically, they are also freestyling on born-again salvation theology.

The inner city harvest is impacted by these surprising trends, because freestyle evangelicals tend to care more about making a difference in their cities than the traditional religious right. Their community values generate concern for the plight of needy families. However, their beliefs about heaven may doctrinally undermine their fervor for proclaiming a clear Gospel message once they become involved in the inner city.

Evangelists should correct this doctrine during their equipping ministries by heightening the connection between spiritual regeneration and eternal life. Not only does the lack of conviction about being born again deny Jesus Christ and every tenant of His Gospel; without the harvest-heaven connection evangelicals lose the urgency of their witness. Why sacrificially spread the Gospel if one believes that other easier options give the same eternal results?

To make a lasting difference, freestyle evangelicals who respond to the call for laborers must bring conviction about the need for spiritual regeneration. Evangelists must equip believers by declaring and clarifying salvation's truth.

I acknowledge that some Christians may experience the new birth without discerning the exact moment of their conversions. For example, Kim and I began explaining the Gospel of Jesus Christ to our four children while they were infants. Throughout their childhoods we exalted the Lord Jesus with each of them during our personal times together and in nightly devotions. We do not recall times when they made special prayers to receive regeneration, but at young ages they put their trust in the Lord and still know Him.

Although the "sinner's prayer" gives an opportunity to express repentance and to call upon the Lord's Name, evangelicals may believe that regeneration can take place without a formal prayer. For example, the Holy Spirit came upon Cornelius, his family and close friends while Peter was still proclaiming of the Gospel to them (Acts 10:44). Nevertheless, according to Christ's own words, new birth certainly occurs when persons believe in Him and remains a necessary experience when eternal life is received (John 3:3-17).

For this reason, evangelists should become concerned that some freestyle evangelicals apparently trust in their church participation or moral lifestyles to get into heaven! My wife Kim grew up going to church and exemplified the family values of "Red State" evangelicals, except she did not realize her need for a spiritual birth.   She believed in the existence of Jesus Christ, knew about his death and resurrection and assumed that she had obeyed enough of His teachings to merit eternal life.

When I explained about her need for a Savior, introduced her to the risen Lord Jesus, showed her from the Bible the purpose of His death on the cross and explained her need to personally give control of her life to Him, she grasped the Gospel of grace. Kim had grown up attending church but was unaware of really how to trust in the Lord Jesus as the One who died on the cross to rescue her from the punishment for her sins.

Since faith must have an object, those serving in the spiritual harvest must present a biblically accurate, clear Gospel. They must invite people to put their faith in the Lord Jesus and become new creations in Him to receive eternal life in heaven. The Lord's powerful Gospel of salvation makes the lasting difference in a person's life.

DNA Analysis

I offer a "DNA analysis" to assess a ministry's state of readiness for mobilization. It gives leaders insights on how to prepare people to support change *before* they begin strategic planning. By using a series of continuums grouped together under the following three headings, **D**esign, **N**eighborliness and **A**ctivism, this analysis summarizes unique spiritual, structural, cultural and historical dynamics that determine a ministry's potential for beginning inner city outreach. The goal here is to prepare ministries to strategically fulfill their missions and not just compose useless statements that sit ineffectually in their filing cabinets.

Instead of picturing biological DNA strands, visualize where your ministry might land on the continuums shown below. Notice how I have concluded that the two dynamics linked by each continuum have an opposite effect on a ministry's ability to build relationships with their inner city neighbors. Those dynamics listed on the left side of the continuums disengage ministries from their neighborhoods while the dynamics listed on the right promote neighborhood evangelism. By assessing a ministry's level of engagement, leaders may help their people move across these continuums to become more involved with their inner city neighbors. These shifts prepare a church, school or outreach ministry to transform its mission to include the inner city.

1. Design Dynamics:

Disengaging	*Engaging*
Programs .... People	
Administration Skills	Giftedness
Program Success	Community
Personnel Management	Discipleship
Professionals............................... Participative	
Hiring	Empowering
Personalities	Priesthood
Outsider Leadership	Indigenous
Prosperity .... Problem Solving	
Comfort Seeking	Self-Sacrificing
Avoiding Conflict	Intervening
Politics .... Purpose	
Controlling	Strategic
Fearing	Faith

The first DNA category, "Design," refers to the structural make-up of a ministry and its mode of operation. When developing a mission statement, leaders of a church or school should identify the dynamics of their current design, pray specifically about them, seek God's supernatural transformation when needed and choose a strategic structure that better engages their people in the inner city harvest.

Programs or People? Effective cross-cultural, inner city evangelism requires ministry structures that make relationships a much greater priority than developing and maintaining **programs**. I believe that program-based churches will become more and more obsolete and ineffective in our **post-modern**, relationship-oriented society because people today value experiencing a sense of community, which is often stifled by programs. Christian leaders should learn how to recognize the differences between these two structural dynamics and assess their position on this continuum before beginning a strategic planning process.

Professionals or Participative? Churches designed for member participation should equip them in **relational evangelism**. This discipleship process provides the foundation for mobilizing their congregations to reach their neighbors for Christ.

In contrast, church members used to hiring professionals to do their outreach for them will probably not cross the many divides that hinder developing lasting, meaningful discipleship relationships in the inner city. Churches designed for outreach will provide discipleship, biblical training, and support to mobilize their members to intervene.

Churches maturing through the equipping ministries of spiritually gifted members have an advantage over churches where members passively follow celebrity leaders.

Prosperity or Problem Solving?　Christians equipped to intervene with hurting people through church body-life outreaches become more prepared to make the sacrifices required in inner city outreach.　Churches designed instead for the comfort of their members or for their personal gain will most likely inadvertently turn their members away from the suffering and spiritual warfare generated by urban evangelism.

Politics or Purpose?　To change the status quo and bring transformation in a church's design, biblical purposes must control the membership's decision-making instead of politics.

2. Neighborliness Dynamics:

Disengaging	*Engaging*
Nostalgia	Neighbors
Living in Past	Merciful
Isolated	Involved
Divided	Welcoming
Inward Focused	Outward Focused
Entrenched	Risk Taking

Nostalgia or Neighbors?　This trade-off describes a church's willingness to let go of past preferences to personally involve members in the low-income neighborhoods surrounding them.　A "nostalgic" church family lives in memories of the past when their congregation thrived as a central part of nearby homogeneous neighborhoods.

As the demographics of neighborhoods change and become low-income and racially diverse, a church with the characteristic of nostalgia refuses to adapt and takes steps to preserve divides.　In contrast, the church with a strong "neighbor" philosophy makes mercy ministry a priority in every area of its design and takes risks to sacrificially establish long-term relationships with families living nearby.

3. Activism Dynamics:

Disengaging	*Engaging*
Accommodating	Action
Maintaining Status Quo	Vision for Change
Avoiding Controversy	Fervor for Justice
Working Within Systems	Initiating Outreach

Accommodation or Action? Accommodation describes church members who believe in only working within existing systems and who avoid making confrontational changes. This word, accommodation, represents church members' tendencies to maintain the status quo, especially when change requires personal sacrifices. Action denotes a church's strong fervor for justice, a high level of energy and a broad vision for change.

A church with DNA that is strategically designed to promote relationships, personal involvement, intervention, discipleship, purpose, neighborliness and action will have the organizational foundation to engage in effective inner city evangelism.

Churches may change their DNA to reach inner city neighborhoods in three ways. First, they may plant churches having DNA's designed for outreach. Similar to church planting, churches or denominations may revitalize congregations in buildings of "nostalgic" churches whose membership rolls declined because they failed to evangelize their new racially and socio-economically different neighbors.

The third option applies to existing, viable churches and ministries. They may transform for inner city outreach by fearlessly evaluating their make-ups and modes of operation, by preparing their people to support change, by implementing strategically planned visions, and by establishing accountability mechanisms to ensure that they stay on course.

Mission Statement Inventory

1. What parts of your ministry's mission statement will have value when you stand before the Book of Life and face Jesus Christ?

2. What opportunities exist for reviewing your ministry's mission statement to consider including the inner city harvest?

3. What obstacles prevent you from transforming your ministry's mission statement?

4. Estimate and circle your ministry's main position on each of the following "DNA" continuums. Connect the circled numbers.

Design Dynamics:

Programs	1	2	3	4	5	People
Professionals	1	2	3	4	5	Participative
Prosperity	1	2	3	4	5	Problem Solving
Personalities	1	2	3	4	5	Priesthood
Politics	1	2	3	4	5	Purpose

Neighborliness Dynamics:

Nostalgia	1	2	3	4	5	Neighbors

Activism Dynamics:

Accommodation	1	2	3	4	5	Action

5. Action Steps: Write a personal mission statement that reflects your own core values. Pray for wisdom to expand this statement as you work through the following chapters of this book.

3 | Expanding Your Vision

At that time Jesus, full of joy through the Holy Spirit, said, "I praise you, Father, Lord of heaven and earth." Luke 10:21 (NIV)

Strategically planned inner city outreach calls for developing a moving vision that produces action and change. Leaders of churches and schools should prayerfully ascertain what they expect their ministries to look like at specific future times, as they include the inner city in their core values and mission statements. Jesus' earthly ministry demonstrated the following four features of a **vision statement** that move people to take action:

1. Start with the lost when developing the vision.
2. Emphasize equipping leaders.
3. Make the vision a joyful investment.
4. Choose developing relationships by extending justice and mercy as the vision's priority.

This chapter highlights the first three of these change-producing forces of a vision statement patterned after Jesus' example. The remaining sections of this book explain how justice, mercy and relationships remain critical to the success of inner city evangelism.

Jesus' Vision Statements Started with the Lost.   Jesus instructed His disciples to plan strategically and He turned their vision toward unbelievers in the spiritual harvest. Refocusing their attention on spiritual values, He even included evangelizing **Samaritans**, who were a race of people treated as outcasts by the Jews. About them Jesus said to His disciples, "Lift up your eyes and look on the fields . . ." (John 4:35). Likewise in Luke 10:2, Jesus commissions evangelists by commanding them to first pray for harvest laborers. Then in Acts 1:7-8, Jesus is about to return to heaven when He redirects His disciples' vision towards becoming His witness to unbelievers. They ask Him about restoring the kingdom to Israel, but Jesus instead commissions them to witness for Him from Jerusalem to the end of the world, through the Holy Spirit's power.

Following Jesus' example, strategic evangelism starts with a concern for the lost. Effective vision for inner city outreach should begin with seeing the potential of spiritual transformation among its families and individuals. This vision includes anticipating the Gospel spreading through impoverished neighborhoods as families are mobilized for evangelistic work at home and abroad. Jesus rejoices in Luke 10:21-22 that this kind of harvest-based vision came from His Father, is hidden from the wise and is now purposefully revealed to Christ's disciples.

This process of creating a vision statement by starting with unbelievers and the spiritual harvest sheds some light on reasons why evangelicals do not include the inner city harvest in their personal, church or school mission statements. Most suburban evangelical Christians have disengaged from the inner city and cannot see the needs and spiritual openness of the families there.

To many Christians, the idea that they have untapped

potential in their churches or schools to minister in the inner city or that they have neglected their responsibilities for urban evangelism remains almost inconceivable. Segregation and the **ghettoization** of the inner city poor prevent them from seeing the ripe harvest.

The action of going out as "disciple-makers," in obedience to Christ's Great Commission in Matthew 28:19, creates the ability to see the harvest and develop strategic vision. Herein is the "Catch 22" regarding inner city evangelism: if middle class evangelical Christians avoid the inner city, they will not acquire the vision for including its harvest in their mission and vision statements.

The opposite is also true. When Kim and I began serving there in 1980, times where such that most white and black Christians in our lives questioned our potential to successfully work with inner city young people. Their skepticism came too late to stop me from being optimistic and full of faith about my vision. By then the Lord had already opened several doors for evangelism with impoverished families. I had already owned the conviction that I had the privilege and potential to successfully include the inner city harvest in my life's mission statement.

Distractions often demobilize evangelicals when they base their vision statements on nonnegotiable traditions or programs instead of starting with a strategic concern for the lost. When evangelists have to work around convenient "**sacred cows**" that eat up valuable resources but do not further the harvest, they usually fail to equip church members to strategically fulfill the mission statement of Jesus.

Since churches have the freedom to organize in ways that most effectively obey Christ's commission, the best vision must come by working back from the evangelization of families to determine how outreaches should be designed.

On several occasions over the years, leaders from different churches and denominations who see their congregations dwindling as their neighborhood demographics change have asked me for advice about how to attract blacks to their services. To check whether their vision for outreach begins with the needs of the lost, I ask if they would be willing to hire a black pastor. More often than not the leaders respond that their people are not yet ready for such a change, which indicates to me that their ministry vision did not begin with the concerns of their unsaved neighbors.

Their planning starts with racial preferences requiring any outreach to bend to their own interests, comforts and conveniences. Members in these churches usually do not live long enough to experience, on this side of heaven, the ready inner city harvest. Tragically, God takes most of them home before their buildings become available for fulfilling the vision of reaching inner city residents with the Gospel.

I will discuss in Chapter 14 Christ's parable of the Good Samaritan. For now I quote Dr. Martin Luther King, Jr. to support starting with the lost to create an action-producing vision:

> **The first question which the priest and the Levite asked was: "If I stop to help this man, what will happen to me?" But... the Good Samaritan reversed the question: "If I do not stop to help this man, what will happen to him?"**[1]

Although I define mercy in Chapter 15, I emphasize here that the truly merciful must consciously focus on others more than themselves. Just as we must keep our gaze on God to be effectual in prayer, we must know and understand the "least of these" to become effective in outreach.

I believe that our enemy often promotes self-centeredness as Christians participate and support outreach ministries. C.S. Lewis warns in *The Screwtape Letters* that the forces of evil seek to undermine the prayers of believers by turning their gaze away from God and towards themselves. Lewis illustrates how Christians may be deceived by Satan to change their prayers into unnoticed processes of manufacturing good feelings about themselves. Instead they should direct them "Not to what I think Thou art but to what Thou knowest Thyself to be." He warns how demons want to influence us to "estimate the value of each prayer by their success in producing a desired feeling."[2]

In the same way, a vision for mercy ministry must begin by focusing on those in need. We must avoid the deception of valuing, organizing or supporting outreaches that just help us feel merciful, righteous or evangelistic without making a lasting difference with the lost. This is such an important statement for church and Christian school leaders to grasp, I am going to repeat myself: we need to avoid the deception of promoting outreaches that just help us to feel merciful but do not make a lasting difference with the lost.

Inherent in Satan's strategy is to blind believers to the self-centeredness and futility of their prayers or outreaches. For this reason, Christians should be wary when fundraisers use emotional appeals to raise support for inner city ministries. To become strategic in giving, donors should give to ministries that consciously know and apply the true meaning of mercy and resist the temptation to make contributions based just on their benefit of generating good feelings.

Jesus' Vision Statement Emphasizes Equipping Leaders.
Ephesians 4:11,12 highlights Jesus' commitment to using gifted persons to equip His workers. He also demonstrated in His earthly ministry a "transformative" leadership development process when He taught, showed, observed and mentored His disciples before pulling them up into leadership roles as His replacements and representatives.[3]

Luke 10 records how Jesus follows this equipping strategy when giving His disciples a community evangelism assignment. He also joyfully praises His Father in this passage for having the vision to equip these improbable workers to fulfill great evangelistic purposes.

Likewise, effective inner city ministry requires a vision for equipping men. Seeing inner city men as potential evangelistic leaders and designing ministries to equip them through transformative leadership development can make inner city ministry successful. Unfortunately, most evangelicals fail to include the equipping of these men in their vision statements and perpetuate injustices that corrupt the Gospel. I will address these problems in Step 2.

Churches who appreciate leadership potential in inner city men will reap eventual growth. When God matures these men and anoints their ministries, they become valuable role models who attract families from like backgrounds and races. Those churches who invest in these men by providing training and ministry opportunities, even while these men are new believers, also make their ministries attractive to other inner city men and their families.

Jesus' Vision Statement Generates Joy. After admonishing His ambassadors to rejoice that their names were written in heaven, Jesus overflows with joy and praise to His Father for choosing and mobilizing the disciples, who originally looked like unlikely evangelists. In Luke 10:21, Jesus, full of joy through the Holy Spirit, exulted: "I thank Thee, O Father, Lord of heaven and earth, that Thou hast hid these things from the wise and prudent, and hast revealed them unto babes: even so it seemed good in Thy sight."

Nowhere else in the New Testament do we find Jesus Christ expressing such joy-filled praise to the Father. In doing so, He proclaims God's pleasure in using the least of men to demonstrate His grace and power. All three members of the Godhead celebrated the supernatural empowerment of the these evangelists.

I first tasted the joy of evangelistic ministry as a young teenager. An African-American **Child Evangelism Fellowship** missionary, Rev. James Earls, took me into slums and public housing neighborhoods in Norfolk and Portsmouth, Virginia, during one of my summer vacations. We shared the gospel with children through Good News Clubs.

This experience of leading children to Christ during the summer mornings transformed my afternoon paper route on those same days. My heart overflowed with joy and songs of praise. Although I did not understand much about praise and worship then, I sang, gave thanks, and prayed while I threw papers. My route seemed to fly by and after finishing I zig-zagged back and forth on my bike in gladness.

Pastor Earls turned me on to the fullness of joy in Jesus' harvest that comes from rejoicing in the Holy Spirit. I became hooked at an early age and have yet to find anything that brings me more joy than seeing people receive the Lord Jesus.

I compare the experience of rejoicing like Jesus to the joy

I felt when watching Kim give birth to each of our four children. My daughter Joanna's birth stands out especially in my mind because of the crisis we endured during it. My joy and praise to God overflowed so much after she escaped a life threatening complication that I actually looked down as I left the hospital to see if my feet were touching the ground. Wow! Childbirth brings that same intense joy that comes from the spiritual harvest. How can we put a price on such joy?

Jesus' words in Luke 10: 24 emphasize the value of laboring in His harvest, ". . . many prophets and kings have desired to see those things which ye see, and have not seen them . . ." We are clearly among the richest people in history. Exulting in the fullness of the Holy Spirit is priceless.

This blessing transcends the cultural, racial and socio-economic divides. The joy God gave me when seeing Jasmine Parker respond to Christ was matched as I introduced another young basketball player and her mother to the Lord. Lizzie Robey, a white middle-class athlete started on my high school junior varsity basketball team in the ninth grade. Although she was just as competitive as Jasmine, she had a gentle spirit and came from a much different background. Her parents, Ed and Shaunna, own a home in Norfolk's affluent Ghent community, where Ed is a urologist.

After practice one afternoon I talked with Lizzie while she sat on a brick fence waiting for her parents to pick her up. She was distressed after receiving a low grade earlier that day.

I took the opportunity to ask about her faith in Christ and tried to clear up some misunderstandings about the Gospel. She quietly said that she understood. In subsequent weeks her relationship with the Lord blossomed as she grew spiritually. At a Fellowship of Christian Athletes leadership camp later that year she wrote in her testimony that she accepted Jesus during our discussion.

Lizzie's strong faith strengthened the friendships between our families. After a few months, I mentioned to the Robeys my interest in starting a Bible study. Her mother Shaunna quickly responded, "I don't do Bible studies." I made her answer a matter of prayer and wondered if something in her past had hardened her heart against the Bible. Perhaps her education had left her skeptical.

After several weeks, the Robeys invited our family over to play "Pictionary." I took advantage of a break in our game-night to ask Shaunna why she refused to participate in Bible studies. Her reasons surprised me. Shaunna explained that her parents had been atheists and had not exposed her to Bible teaching. She said that she felt embarrassed in Bible studies because she could not find references and did not understand anything discussed.

Trying to hide my excitement, I related to Shaunna how my ministry centered on explaining the Bible to persons in the inner city who have little or no knowledge of its teachings. I made her a promise that I could unlock the Bible in six lessons, if she would give me the opportunity. Our families began meeting together on Sunday evenings and we invited two high school friends of our teenagers and their mother, Dee Page.

Shaunna put her faith in Jesus Christ after our second lesson. I asked if anyone wanted to surrender control of his or her life to the Lord. Shaunna immediately and boldly spoke up in front of our families and said, "I do. I believe that Jesus Christ is my Lord and Savior." The rest of us sat stunned by joy!

Knowing and coaching Jasmine and Lizzie felt extremely rewarding, but being used by God to lead them and their family members to eternal life remains priceless in my mind. Although they came to Christ from different backgrounds and circumstances, they became a part of the same spiritual harvest that resulted in joyful praise to God.

The following account of a wise investment illustrates part of my motivation for mobilizing workers for this spiritual inner city harvest. I know someone who bought high-risk stocks in a new technology company. The company flourished and its stock price soared so this investment paid off extremely well. Because this person's vision and counsel convinced several friends to take the same risk, they all reaped the same extraordinary financial reward.

Years later, the son of one of these fortunate friends visited this wise investor to express thanks for his foresight and advice. The grateful young man's father had used the stock's return to pay for this son's college and law school expenses.

Similarly, I have invested my life in a risky ministry venture and struck the "mother load" of spiritual joy. By casting a vision based on Christ's principles, I want to convince others to join me in this harvest and reap this same amazing grace and eternal blessing of rejoicing with our Lord.

Vision Inventory

1.   In what ways has God broadened your vision for inner city evangelism?

2.   Write your ministry's vision statement:

3.   What components of your ministry's vision originate from concern for spiritually lost neighbors?

4.   What components of this vision statement preserve nonnegotiable traditions or preferences?

5.   Which of these components of Jesus' vision statement need to be strengthened in your ministry's vision?
___   Start with the lost when developing the vision
___   Emphasize equipping leaders
___   Make the vision a joyful investment
___   Choose developing relationships through extending justice and mercy as the vision's priority

6.   Action Step:
Organize a prayer ride through local inner city neighborhoods to identify their names and witness their plights. Add their names to your prayer journal.

Step 2

Understanding the Spiritual History and Environment

And He said to them, "I beheld Satan as lightning falling from heaven." Luke 10:18

4 | Disarming the Enemy

In sports, there is nothing better than a great comeback. I find my most exhilarating experiences when coaching basketball occurring in the fourth quarters of our games, especially during a time out when my team is coming back from a deficit. I challenge my players at those critical moments to embrace the triumph by stopping our opponent through aggressive defense and by taking control of the game using a deliberate offense.

The greater the deficit at first, the more fun the comeback becomes to us. Looking into their eyes as I shout instructions over the pandemonium caused by the pep band and cheerleaders, I encourage them to enjoy this predicament because this kind of pressure and competition is what the game is all about.

As you read the chapters in this section about the spiritual warfare associated with the inner city harvest, you will discover that evangelicals have been losing horribly to the Evil One for almost half a millennium. The good news is that we currently find ourselves in the fourth quarter and on a comeback.

Know Your Enemy

Deadly warfare from Satan and his evil forces is a spiritual reality taught in Scripture. Revelation 12:17 exposes the Devil's hatred of God's people and his declaration of war against those who keep the Lord's commandments and witness for Jesus Christ.

When seeking to understand the inner city's spiritual environment and history, remember that we do not wrestle against flesh and blood but against the rulers of darkness in this world (Eph. 6:12). Notice the ways the Evil One undermines believers' testimonies and fosters disobedience by alienating us from the truth that extending mercy and justice should be our first priorities when seeking to obey the Great Commission.

As you read on about Christ's commission to show mercy, prepare yourself to discover how Satan also tempts Christians with an impotent, counterfeit mercy. He also camouflages injustices by embedding them as destructive hidden sins in systems, structures and institutions. Satan uses these failures to infiltrate and divide the spiritual harvesters.

Keep in the mind that the weapons of our warfare come from God who tears down the spiritual strongholds created by our invisible opponents as we use these weapons properly. The Lord of the Harvest has enlisted us in this serious spiritual conflict and He has provided the weapons to successfully overcome the enemy.

Let us know our enemy, learn how to use spiritual weapons and embrace the triumph that we possess in Christ. Like coming back from a sports injury, we may need to spend time with our Trainer to strengthen feeble arms and weak knees (Heb. 12:12 NIV). Nevertheless, the losses of the past will make our victory sweet as we take our stand.

The eight chapters in this second step explain the tactics of our evil opponent and how to stop him. Later chapters explain how to win.

Since effective strategic planners must understand historical backgrounds and adapt to environmental opportunities, threats and changes, those who desire to enter the inner city's spiritual battlefield ought to have their hearts open for introspection and repentance. Christians who know the spiritual history and environment of the inner city will become more effective in making lasting changes.

Evil Tactics

Of Satan's fiery darts opposing the Christ and inflicting pain on His believers, the worst must include destroying the Gospel's credibility, preventing the bold witness of Christ's commissioned ones, and polluting the clarity of their message. The Apostle Paul rarely asks for prayer except that he might proclaim the mystery of Christ clearly and fearlessly, as he should (Col. 3:11; Eph. 6:19). The spiritual forces of evil strive in this world to corrupt God's simple message of salvation and to immobilize believers with feelings of fear that may prevent us from going out as commanded.

In Ephesians 4:25, God's Word commands us to speak truthfully and handle anger correctly to prevent giving Satan an open door to implement his divisive schemes: "Therefore each of you must put off falsehood and speak truthfully to his neighbor, for we are all members of one body. 'In your anger do not sin.' Do not let the sun go down while you are still angry, and do not give the devil a foothold"(NIV).

Racism provides the enemy many divisive footholds to support his dastardly war against the clear Gospel. For the sake of Christ and His Gospel, let us take a "fearless moral inventory" of Christian racism and speak truthfully about black and white racial reconciliation.

Although many in society are tired of trying to understand and solve racial problems, Christians may overcome this racial fatigue by making Christ's spiritual harvest the higher, overarching goal for crossing racial divides.[1]   Commitment to ending racism should increase after evangelicals comprehend how its historical and present-day occurrences damage the Gospel's credibility.

An Example from Jamaica

To understand how the Evil One alienates many from the Gospel, consider the devastating spiritual impact of white racism on persons of African descent. I write this chapter after returning from a missions trip to Jamaica in 2004. We partner with a circuit of Jamaican churches to mobilize persons of African descent for world missions, which I explain in my first book *Reconciling an Oppressor*.[2]

On one particular day of this trip, a twenty-three year old Jamaican young man named Dean Vale, and a twenty-one year old African-American female intern with our ministry, Courtney Haywood, ventured out with me into the town of Buff Bay. God used our friendships to tear down spiritual strongholds built on past white racism, oppression and segregated missions.

Dean took us to visit a Rasta, a local Jamaican leader in the Rastafarian religion, who sold souvenirs at wholesale prices. This short, thin man appeared worn down by the elements. He had few teeth and kept his distinguishing dreadlocks in an old wrap on his head. The Rasta had his wares spread across a blanket on the cement steps of the town's small, curb-side post office. He explained that as a true Rasta, he avoided manipulating tourists through the popularization of Rastafarian dress, music and marijuana.

Dean spoke up after I had purchased some gifts to take

home to my family. He said, "*Mike, tell 'im what's you're about in Jamaica.*" The Rasta looked at me with curiosity, so I replied, "The reason that I am here is Jesus Christ."

This answer caught the Rasta so off guard that I thought he might fall off the post office steps. Jesus was the last person whom he thought this strong Jamaican young man, an African-American young lady and this gray-haired white man would bring up. The Rasta raised his arms in surprise.

The Lord gave me the opportunity to listen and to agree with him about the injustices that the Jamaicans have endured from white followers of Christ. He asked me why I had come to Jamaica, which has more churches per square mile than any other country in the world.

I sat down next to him on the post office porch and answered with a question, "Why did men in the Jamaican mountains call me an oppressor?" The Rasta respectfully answered, "Do you know that white missionaries used Christianity to oppress? White people used the Bible to make people submit to slavery."

I admitted to the Rasta the past and present sin of white Christian racism and emphasized that Jesus did not condone this oppression. I explained that our team (Jamaican, African-American, and white) wanted to explain the truth about Jesus Christ with justice. My willingness to acknowledge white injustices and my friendships with Dean and Courtney created a bond of acceptance with this man.

Although his religion capitalizes on the sins of white missionaries to discredit Christianity and to turn Jamaicans away from Christ, I could tell that our Gospel message cut deep into this man's heart. I believe that we broke through a stronghold of bitterness that Satan had perpetrated through white racism.

Disarming the spiritual enemies of the Gospel of Jesus Christ begins by removing the footholds of division within evangelical Christianity that Satan has established to drive a wedge between the races. White evangelicals may start with a fearless moral inventory of how the evil one uses feelings of racial superiority, economic evangelism, domination evangelism, paternalistic evangelism, racial segregation, division of good doctrine and misuse of a missions strategy to undermine the mobilization of laborers for the spiritual harvest in the inner city.

Spiritual Warfare Inventory

1. In what ways have you engaged in spiritual warfare for the salvation of inner city families?
2. What factors in your ministry support spiritual warfare in evangelism?
3. What detracts from effective spiritual warfare?
4. How have you improved your understanding of the spiritual divides undermining the Gospel in the inner city?

5. Action Steps:
Ask a prayer partner to intercede for you as you take on the introspection coming in the next chapters of this section.
Ask God for wisdom to reveal and destroy any footholds that Satan has established in your life and ministry.

---

5 | Feeling Racially Superior

Twenty years ago I became convicted by the following accusation of Peter Bergman in his book *History of the American Negro*:

> . . . racial superiority - a fallacy in which even Martin Luther and Thomas More believed. These church reformers supported the idea that slavery was a necessary social institution and thus even humanitarian-minded and educated Englishmen lost shame and conscience in their views of the Negro.[1]

If Bergman's assertion is true, then the modern church has never been without this root of wickedness of whites feeling superior to blacks and other races. The devil has used this spiritual stronghold and false doctrine to corrupt the gospel for almost five centuries.

Indeed, feelings of **racial superiority** perpetuated and caused multiplied injustices through generations of conservative Christians since the days of the **Reformers** in the 16th century. So ingrained was this thinking that white theologians debated for a century whether Africans even had souls or not! This debate did not include other races.

To end this foothold of Satan, white Christians need to

recognize the prevalence and deadly consequences of past **racial prejudice**, repent when it prevails today and act justly to bring reconciliation and healing. Although my book does not intend to debate issues associated with slavery, I believe that white Christians must become aware of how prejudiced feelings of racial superiority fostered false doctrines that blacks were pre-destined to serve whites.

> **It was argued that the Negro was inferior by nature because of Noah's curse upon the children of Ham . . . The greatest blasphemy of the whole ugly process was that the white man ended up making God his partner in the exploitation of the Negro. Dr. Martin Luther King, Jr.[2]**

Whites did not invent slavery and today cannot control what happened in the past, but to prevent allowing feelings of racial superiority from prevailing in Christian practices we must seek to comprehend how racist biblical teaching produced deadly consequences for tens of millions of enslaved Africans.

During the trans-Atlantic slave trade racial prejudice excused the death of slaves caused by executions, disease, exhaustion and starvation. Other slaves died during mutinies and by suicide. Thousands more perished due to the treacher-ous conditions whites forced slaves to live under in America.

Even after the Civil War, whites, with the belief of racial superiority, lynched over 5,000 blacks under the cover of **Jim Crow** laws. White churches put racial segregation in their con-stitutions, some actually ending services when black persons tried to attend.

By 1925, the **Klu Klux Klan** (KKK) with its doctrine of

white supremacy, had recruited over 40,000 pastors from large denominations. Many of these became officials, leading whole communities into the Klan.[3] Even northern white churches implemented violent racial segregation policies, though removed from the direct influences of the KKK because it flourished mostly in the south.

Attitudes of racial superiority prevail today as footholds for Satan to widen the divide between the blacks and whites. Unfortunately, feeling racially superior contributes to the white perception that past injustices were inconsequential, which keeps alive hurts that black feel from past. When whites see the many opportunities given to African-Americans, some wonder why blacks cannot just get over the past and get on with their lives. Evangelicals should be the most wary about this foothold because racial prejudice had the power to create false doctrines that allowed past injustices to occur.

Sociologists have identified an association between evangelical beliefs and racial prejudice. They conclude from studies that Americans who are most likely to racially and ethnically discriminate are church members who believe in the essentials of evangelical doctrine. This correlation has been so strong that researchers even investigate and debate whether evangelical teachings actually cause racial prejudice. (Many persons of African descent from around the world conclude that these two factors are causally related. They have experienced **racial discrimination** from whites who represent the evangelical Christian faith, they see only historically **paternalistic** white missionaries and they hear accusations from some of their own spiritual leaders that Christianity is an oppressive white man's religion.)

Studies also show that spiritual commitment impacts the correlation between evangelicalism and prejudice. Church members with marginal levels of commitment to their faith are more prejudiced than committed church members.[4] Again the question of cause and effect arises. Does the lack of spiritual commitment increase the tendency for racial prejudice or would harboring racial prejudice contribute to spiritual coldness?

Regardless of the reasons for these associations between prejudice and evangelical beliefs, the mere existence of these well-known correlations exposes systemic sin among us.

The late African-American evangelist, Tom Skinner, addressed Urbana 70 (the largest missions conference held in the U.S. and sponsored by Inter Varsity Christian Fellowship at the University of Illinois) and gave these details about the history of evangelical racism in slavery:

> **You must keep in mind that, during this period of time, in general (there were some notable exceptions, but in general) the evangelical, Bible-believing, fundamental, orthodox, conservative church in this country was strangely silent. In fact, there were those people who during slavery argued, "It's not our business to become involved in slavery. That is a social issue. We have been called to preach the gospel. We must deliver the Word. We must save people's souls. We must not get involved in the issues of liberating people from the chains of slavery. If they accept Jesus Christ as their Savior, by and by they will be free - over there."**
>
> **To a great extent the evangelical church in America supported the status quo. It supported slavery; it supported segregation; it preached against any attempt of the black man to stand on**

his own two feet. And where there were those who sought to communicate the gospel to black people, it was always done in a way to make sure that they stayed cool. "We will preach the gospel to those folks so they won't riot; we will preach the gospel to them so that we can keep the lid on the garbage pail."

And so they were careful to point out such scriptures as: "Obey your masters," "Love your enemy," "Do good to them that hurt you." But no one ever talked about a message, which would also speak to the oppressor.[5]

Drs. C. Everett Koop and Francis Schaeffer warned evangelicals in the 1980's that viewing human beings as non-persons leads to violent injustices. They compare the prejudice against blacks during slavery to the views of today's abortion advocates.[6] Christians must seriously confront any attitudes of racial superiority that prevail today.

The devil's proven strategy of using racial prejudice to destroy the credibility of the Gospel has become subtle but is just as spiritually destructive in the inner city as past injustices. We begin tearing down this stronghold by confessing sins rooted in feelings of superiority. This requires a fearless inventory of our personal beliefs, doctrines, values and attitudes, as well as our structures and methodologies.

Shout it aloud, do not hold back. Raise your voice like a trumpet. Declare to my people their rebellion and to the house of Jacob their sins. For day after day they seek me out; eager to know my ways, as if they were a nation that does what is

right and has not forsaken the commands of its God. They ask for just decisions and seem eager for God to come near them . . . Is not the kind of fasting I have chosen: to loose the chains of injustice and untie the chords of the yoke, to set the oppressed free and break every yoke (Isaiah 58:1-2 and 6 NIV)?

After almost five centuries of this racist corruption in our witness to persons of African descent, should we not expect an outpouring of the Spirit of God when the Gospel is preached with attitudes of repentance demonstrated by works of justice? These works will be explained in later chapters.

Racial Superiority Inventory

1.   What are the underlying attitude differences between these two kinds of evangelism philosophies? "Let's invite them to come here and understand us." "Go and learn to understand them."
2.   What precautions have you and your leadership taken to prevent allowing the sin of whites feeling racially superior over blacks to corrupt your ministry's values?
3.   Have feelings of racial superiority established a foothold in your ministry in any ways?
4.   Action Step: Spend time before the Lord in confession and repentance for personal and corporate sins rooted in prideful feelings of racial superiority.

6 | Economic Evangelism

The foothold of **economic evangelism** becomes evident when strategies of justice and mercy are pursued only if they are financially feasible and when evangelism depends on whether an outreach makes good business sense.

For example, the Gospel of Jesus Christ created a dilemma for white colonists when they assumed that they would have to free those slaves who accepted Christ and became baptized. As a result, slaveholders avoided evangelizing their slaves to prevent economic losses. The following law resolved the dilemma created by the Gospel:

> **Virginia Statute ACT III 16667/09**
> **baptism of slaves doth not exempt them from bondage.**[1]

Once this new law preserved the economic benefit of owning Christian slaves, the slave owners began evangelizing their slaves. This law also gave whites the opportunity to distort Bible passages to teach Christian slaves to submit.

During the next two centuries most Southern pastors made similar economic decisions every Sunday. They failed to preach against slavery and segregation because they would lose their jobs and church members. In the South, the desire for church growth overrode the desire for justice.   Methodist churches are representative of what occurred in other denominations.   Although John Wesley had denounced slavery, Southern Wesleyans eventually overlooked the injustices of slavery to grow their church memberships.[2]

The violent oppression by whites against blacks during Jim Crow created a marketing dilemma for evangelists who wanted to use revivals to save the souls of whites. If these evangelists took a stand against segregation, lynchings and racial discrimination, then whites would not attend their meetings and miss hearing the Gospel.   Dwight L. Moody avoided this problem by purposely segregating his revivals and his speaking itineraries in the South. He also remained silent about the oppression of lynch mobs that terrorized African-Americans into submission to unjust laws and ghettos.[3]

Likewise, evangelist Charles Finney, although he had laid groundwork for abolishing slavery, later rejected it when he concluded that the abolition movement was a detriment to evangelism.   He condoned racial prejudice and segregation to avoid raising issues that prevented conversions and unity in white congregations.

As a result, prejudice and segregation remained acceptable to evangelicals of the North even as some called for the end of slavery. This thinking paved the way for the silent neglect of African-Americans by white evangelicals during the horrible injustices of Jim Crow, which occurred when slavery ended.[4]

This methodology prevails today through homogeneous church growth philosophies that perpetuate segregation. One example of this is when for the sake of church growth, churches target a particular race or socio-economic class.   These churches provide special events, meetings and buildings designed to attract a race or class of people by helping them feel comfortable and safe with their own kind and cultures. This goal of homogenous church growth most often results in segregated worship.

Even philanthropy gives Satan a foothold if Christians limit their giving to causes that benefit themselves, their businesses and their families. Donors may miss important causes that promote justice and mercy because many effective strategies for changing inner cities are expensive, labor intensive and, therefore, the least attractive to major donors. Proclaiming the Gospel of Jesus Christ to inner city adults, church planting, discipleship, and Christian education usually are difficult to sell to persons who look for rewards in this life.

Economic considerations have been the driving force in the way society chooses solutions for the plight of the impoverished in modern times. For example, during the **Great Migration** of African-Americans to northern cities, whites sought protection from the economic problems brought by the influx of impoverished blacks. They used housing discrimination and public housing projects to preserve their middle-class, segregated lifestyles by creating black ghettos. White Christians lived in these cities and condoned this segregation, even as black Christians moved into these ghettos and worshiped there.

Though the malice of the past may be gone, I believe that many white churches continue to *ghettoize* along economic lines and consequently hurt the Gospel's impact in the inner city today. Homogeneous church growth strategies still condone targeting persons of a specific race or class for membership while superficially addressing the needs of the poor through missionary support, special programs and seasonal events.

These strategies maintain segregation as the status quo in

the church just as housing ghettoization maintained it in our cities. Programs designed to bring middle-class persons to facilities reduces evangelism to just programmed events rather than relationship-based outreaches, which more effectively connect with inner city families.

An article in *Christianity Today* magazine (August 7, 2000) quotes sociologist Christian Smith's analysis of event-based evangelism as: "A lot of this is evangelicals affirming their identity rather than having a lasting effect."[5] I believe that his analysis also describes many mercy outreaches that churches are involved in as well. As I explained in Chapter 3, church members may feel more like compassionate followers of Christ by implementing temporary, convenient and economically feasible ways to serve the poor from within their facilities.

Supporting urban missionaries, responding to benevolence requests, giving Thanksgiving and Christmas baskets, sponsoring soup kitchens, and organizing mentoring, tutorial and athletic programs can address poverty without encouraging church members to get personally involved in significant ways with the poor and their problems.

Churches often choose to work with these types of programs because they are easier to fund and give apparently quick results. But again, as we mentioned earlier are they really impacting the people there with the true Gospel and love of God? How is the Church different here than other secular organizations?

Furthermore, with crack cocaine destroying so many families, those who serve in these benevolence programs must be careful not to automatically remove the consequences of drug abuse and thereby **enable** addicts to continue in self-destructive behaviors.

I believe that because such programs are easy to start and fund, they often serve the churches more than the inner city families. Real solutions to inner city problems require labor-intensive discipleship interventions that target entire families and that necessitate long-term, sacrificial investments of time and money.

Ironically, missionaries and/or evangelists calling for this level of true intervention and integration often become quickly ghettoized along with the poor. This especially occurs when churches send the workers money but do not become strategically involved in the lives of inner city families.

Other areas of Christian ministry divide similarly along economic lines. Understanding the financial constraints facing Christian schools, we should openly say that **Christian education**, though beneficial for many, is unaffordable for most inner city families. Though founded on the conviction that children need quality Christian education, the vast majority of Christian schools do not include the urban poor in their missions.

The primary reason is money. Tuition and transportation expenses require most families to make financial sacrifices to enroll their own children. Therefore, providing Christian education for the poor seems out of the question to most Christian schools. Although some with this mission exist, the children from just one large public housing neighborhood would financially swamp most of them. There may be many valid reasons for parents to leave the public schools but mercy or justice for the poor is not one of them.

If churches and Christian schools want to take Christian families out of the public schools while pursuing justice for the poor, why not require it in their missions? To achieve certification, let Christian schools demonstrate the ways they make their education affordable for inner city children.

If the dividing line remains an economic one, calling out Christian families from public schools perpetuates injustices and is not Christ-like at all. Recruiting a limited number of middle class minority students and a few public school minority athletes helps make a school appear more diverse and win more games but resembles tokenism and exploitation.

Jesus taught that His followers need to learn what it means to show mercy and it should be a fundamental component of Christian school education.

When finances become the barrier that prevents the Christian poor from attending Christian schools, this barrier also prevents students on both sides from learning a valuable lesson about mercy.

Our wonderful inheritance as God's people includes the opportunity to sacrifice resources to include the poor while trusting Him to supply our own needs. The Lord promises to make all grace abound to those who sacrificially break the yoke of injustice so we have everything needed for every good work.

> **If you spend yourselves in behalf of the hungry and satisfy the needs of the oppressed, then your light will rise in the darkness and your night will become like noonday. The Lord will guide you always; he will satisfy your needs in a sun-scorched land and will strengthen your frame. You will be like a well-watered garden, like a spring whose waters never fail (Is. 58:10-11 NIV).**

Our claim on these promises makes a vision for including inner city children in the Christian school movement reasonable. Including the poor into our schools' mission statements and working diligently to achieve this mission will teach our children justice, mercy and faithfulness. Trusting God for the resources to solve the educational crisis in the inner city should be looked upon as our privilege.

We defy our Lord's command to love our neighbors as ourselves if we sacrificially provide Christian schooling for our own but forsake the poor for financial reasons. If Christian education is biblical, then we must attempt to make it affordable for the poor. Unless Christian schools implement this vision for educating the poor, forsaking our public schools provides the Devil a foothold for alienating families who are unable to afford Christian education.

Increasing racial diversity in Christian schools creates opportunities for all students to apply and celebrate Christian values that may otherwise be left to mere intellectual assent. A core operative in Christian education is the teachers' inclusion of biblical principles into their lessons. Through creative teaching, racial diversity may highlight the following Christian values:

I Peter 2:9	All believers in Jesus Christ are God's chosen race.
I Cor.12:12-13	All believers are baptized by one Spirit into one body.
John 17:20-23	Unity among believers is the will of God and an important part of our testimony.
Rev. 7:9,10	Reconciled racial unity brings God the greatest glory and races worshipping together characterizes heaven.
Rom. 6:23a	The consequence of sin, including racism, is death.

| Matt. 9:23 | **Christ makes showing mercy through relationships a priority in our faith.** |
| Micah 6:8 | **God loves mercy and justice and requires that we extend them to others, especially to those less fortunate than ourselves.** |

When teaching the above biblical values, Christian educators may include justice and mercy in their lessons by taking the following steps:

1. Openly reject racism as sin. Without laying guilt trips and creating bitterness, expose the oppression of whites against blacks and other races, emphasizing forgiveness and repentance for any feelings of superiority or hatred.
2. Teach activism by encouraging students to stand against unjust laws and practices.
3. Proclaim the Gospel's power to reconcile.
4. Show students how to discern prejudice and **ethnocentrism**.
5. Celebrate cultural diversity through the Great Commission.

Even though many congregations especially in metropolitan areas are made up of people from many ethnic backgrounds, there are still many areas in the country where most churches are still segregated. Christian schools drawing racially different families may demonstrate racial reconciliation better than these churches. By partnering with parents to celebrate cultural diversity, Christian educators may also help students of African, Hispanic or Asian descent develop healthy racial identities without necessitating that they **assimilate** into white culture. This context of racial reconciliation and development increases the schools' potential for effectively serving families from inner city backgrounds.

Those persons governing predominantly white Christian schools must accept their responsibility to change structures that keep them limited to white students. Every school may have unique variables that impact its racial diversity. Identifying and removing structural barriers to inner city students are acts of justice.

These changes may disrupt the status quo and require the school's administration, faculty, parents and students to make sacrifices to cross the racial and socio-economic divides that exist between Christian schools and inner city families. Changing structures to open Christian education to the poor teaches students much more about Christ's compassion than sponsoring annual Christmas food drives.

Economic Evangelism Inventory

1. What inner city outreaches would your ministry seek to implement if you could financially afford them?

2. What programs in your ministry do not take into account inner city families because of limited resources?

3. Describe the kind of person your ministry targets for growth. Has adopting a homogeneous church growth strategy excluded inner city families from being targeted by your ministry's evangelism?

4. Action Step: Meet with a Christian school board member and discuss the potential for making the school more affordable to families having low incomes.

7 | Domination Evangelism

Throughout the centuries, some Christian groups have approved of conquering, colonizing and enslaving peoples as means of evangelization. Gaining converts by overpowering and governing is rooted in feelings of superiority. By taking a "fearless moral inventory," we must question whether this value remains in our hearts today, lest we give the Devil another foothold to divide us.

For example, how often do our churches pray for and reach out to the young men who hang out on the streets of our inner cities. Do we view them as feared enemies who we must subdue? Are we quick to assume that they will reject our message? Do we offer programs limited to their women and children, acting as if these men do not exist? Do we bring them the Gospel only after they have been conquered and incarcerated?

At Urban Discovery Ministries, our non-profit, inner city outreach ministry in Norfolk, Virginia, we readjust our own perceptions of the men in the community before we go out to share the Gospel. We remind ourselves to see these men as potential elders and missionaries. We begin community evangelism by approaching men on the streets to show respect and to explain what we intend to accomplish.

We, in effect, request their support in reaching their neighborhood for Christ, explaining that God wants them to become its spiritual leaders. We also explain that God is holding them responsible for bringing their families and neighbors to Christ and that we can never replace them. We ask them for ideas. Whenever God opens a door for evangelism, we look for ways to connect with men. There is a difference between tough love and conquering evangelism. The difference is in how we see and value adult men who need the Gospel.

Even good intentions become hurtful when we forget to respect men who have become embittered by the conflict between the races. How many mission teams send construction workers into the inner city or to impoverished countries while neglecting the plight of unemployed men who watch from the roadsides? (On your next missions building project, try taking less workers. Instead, raise additional support to hire unemployed men to work side by side with your team. Be ready for a wonderful witness for Christ.) Avoiding and opposing inner city men, except during their incarceration, is unjust. Jesus never intended for us to conquer and govern others as a means to spread the Christian faith.

Nothing destroyed faith in evangelical doctrine among African-Americans more than white conquering evangelism, again meaning trying to convert people by overpowering and governing them. This form of white oppression created the offenses that caused many black power leaders to split with evangelical doctrine in the late 60's, when theologians like James Cone began making **Black Experience** the foundation of theology. The offense evoked a militant response from blacks seeking freedom, justice and respect.

The following quote describes how Cone felt and reasoned during this time period:

I vividly remember when I sat down at my desk in Adrian College (Adrian, Michigan) in the wake of the Newark and Detroit riots in July 1967. I could hardly contain my rage against the white church and its theology for their inability to see that the God of Jesus was at work in places they least expected – Black Power! That essay was the beginning of my theological journey. I was well aware of the risk I was taking in making such a radical break with my theological education. But with black people dying in the streets of America, I just could not keep silent.[1]

Black Power became the answer to white conquering evangelism. Every white Christian should study and understand not only the horrors of white oppression but also the devastating spiritual consequences that occurred from the neglect and silence of white evangelical believers during slavery, the Jim Crow era and the ghettoization of our cities. Our forefathers' cruelty and neglect stockpiled almost five centuries of hurts that fueled this black power movement, which began in the sixties.

Since evangelical doctrine demands the empowering of all peoples for the harvest of the Gospel, white evangelicals should have laid down their lives (and should be doing it now) for the equipping of blacks for world evangelization. Jesus Christ, in our infallible Bibles, commands that we serve our neighbors to make for Him disciples of all nations but most white evangelicals have failed to obey this command. Unfortunately, this neglect caused many blacks to forsake the Lord of Justice and turn to *any means necessary* to win freedom and respect.

The effects of Black Power permeated Christianity and deepened the racial divide in the body of Christ. After the Civil War, white Christians began starting expansive ministries for blacks while maintaining governing power over these outreaches. When Black Power arrived in the 1960's, it created such a backlash that the pendulum swung in the opposite direction. Blacks removed entire white missions board members to assume control of their own ministries.

In Africa, white missionaries had governed blacks with the same kind of paternalism for most of the 20th Century. Promises to turn over the governance of their churches to Africans never materialized because white missionaries never deemed them to be ready. After decades of such injustices, Africans followed the advice of Black Power proponents from the States and threw off the control of white missionaries. The failure of white missionaries to empower black leaders caused racial division to thrive on both continents.

Domination Evangelism Inventory

1. What percentage of your ministry's resources are spent on evangelizing, discipling, training and mobilizing inner city young men?

2. Would your ministry classify public housing as a mission field or an untapped source of missionaries?

3. Besides during incarceration, how would men in your city's public housing hear a clear presentation of the gospel?

4. Action Step: Drive through a public housing neighborhood on a nice Sunday afternoon or attend an inner city high school or recreation event. Evaluate your feelings about the young men whom you see. Pray for an open door to introduce them to Jesus Christ.

8 | Paternalistic Evangelism

In the years leading up to the Civil War, the *Charleston Mercury* newspaper defended slavery as "a charitable Christian cause that kept intellectually and morally inferior blacks out of harm's way and provided for their needs."[1] I noticed this mentality on one of my many field trips to Colonial Williamsburg that I took while growing up in Hampton Roads, Virginia. People dressed in sixteenth-century attire hosted tours in its restored homes and shops and explained the historical backgrounds of the colonists who had lived and worked there.

One tour guide showed actual extensive records kept by the wife of a wealthy plantation homeowner. Like other wives of means at that time, her primary work responsibility focused on the care of the slaves and she maintained detailed records of everything she provided them.

This aspect of colonial culture must been have passed on through the generations. I still encounter whites motivated to help in our ministry because their parents taught them that each white person's Christian duty is to help to take care of unfortunate people. For example, such a philosophy might motivate a white person to stop, out of Christian duty, and help a black person with car trouble, while otherwise practicing racial segregation in their personal relationships, community or churches.

Sensing a duty to help take care of another race may

seem like Christian mercy but such teaching is rooted in feelings of racial superiority and smacks of oppression. Called **racial paternalism**, this kind of outreach rightly offends, and sometimes cripples, the disadvantaged.

True Christian duty requires believers to empower the impoverished, not to take care of them like slaves or children. Servant leadership means we equip the poor to take places of honor in the land (I Samuel 2:8). This duty also requires us to train leaders who not only govern themselves, but who can govern the Church as well. We must teach them to obey Christ's Great Commission by giving them a sense of destiny as world disciple makers. Persons living in poverty are not just our mission field; they are our source of missionaries. Christ's justice requires His people to empower and mobilize all believers, regardless of race or socio-economic background, for local and world evangelization.

In the States, Christians implement paternalistic strategies using the poor as objects of annual Christian charity projects and few here recognize the potential of inner city families for world evangelization. Their backgrounds prepare them for effective international missions.

Christians from the inner city already know how to cope with having dual identities - being both minorities and Americans. They have also learned how to be resilient in poverty and in unjust circumstances. They can speak boldly to the poor about fulfilling family, church and community responsibilities because as missionaries coming from the inner city they had to make similar choices. Many have compensated for not receiving adequate education and have persevered through unemployment or low wages, so they can empathize with the poor while calling them to sacrificially obey Christ. I have seen persons from the inner city quickly win the trust of Jamaicans.

To avoid paternalism in the inner city harvest, Christianity needs new strategies for equipping and mobilizing inner city persons for local and foreign missions and for church leadership. These strategies must innovatively empower them to overcome the financial and educational barriers that these persons face in their urban cultural situations.[2] Churches, mission agencies and Bible schools should create new ways for them to achieve biblical training and raise support. The new strategies should also promote partnerships with mature ministries to raise and disperse financial resources without perpetuating paternalistic charity for the poor.

New believers from the inner city must be placed under the Great Commission and empowered to become self-supporting, self-governing and reproducing. These self-initiatives require new church structures and new **discipleship** strategies that rapidly mobilize African-Americans for the global Great Commission. I believe that this mobilization is great justice.

Paternalism Inventory

1. Can you think of examples when you tried to take care of poor individuals?

2. How did you empower them to provide for themselves and to take responsibility for their own wellbeing?

3. How did you enable their dependency on you?

4. Action Steps: Evaluate your dealings with impoverished persons to end or prevent paternalism.
Ask for advice and accountability from other believers when assisting impoverished families to avoid paternalistic benevolence.

9 | Racial Segregation

To say that the Devil has used white Christian **racial segregation** as a foothold to destroy the credibility of the Gospel might be the understatement of the past five centuries. Even though we are only a little more than one generation removed from the era when racial segregation was deemed normal, God-ordained and scriptural, the ignorance of evangelical whites today about segregation's devastating spiritual consequences still surprises me. This sin caused, and still causes, many to defame the precious name of the Lord Jesus Christ and reject the truth of His Gospel.

The same **fundamentalists** who fought passionately to protect the essentials of our faith and defend the Word of God from attacks by **liberal** theologians dishonored God and the Gospel by racially segregating their families, churches and Bible colleges. In contrast, liberal colleges and seminaries began to open their doors to racial integration after the Civil War and have taught social justice from then until now.

During **Reconstruction** in the South following the Civil War, theologically liberal **abolitionists** provided funding for black colleges and evidently influenced their doctrine. In our Hampton Roads, Virginia, metropolitan area, Hampton University's history illustrates the losses to evangelical Christianity resulting from segregation. Booker T. Washington graduated from Hampton Institute, which later became this Hampton University, during a time when the college existed to educate and evangelize African-Americans. Hampton Institute's charter asserted that its "teaching should always be evangelical." The son of missionary parents, Brigadier General Samuel Chapman Armstrong founded Hampton Institute, which made Hampton an oasis of opportunity for the thousands of newly freed blacks gathered behind Union lines.[1] His tests of faith were reality, loyalty and efficiency.

> **Among his most loyal friends were Quakers from Philadelphia and Unitarians from Boston; and when the question was raised by cautious observers whether these gifts might not affect injuriously the orthodoxy of the school, whose charter had determined that its 'teaching should be evangelical,' Armstrong's reply was unequivocal. 'The Institute must have a positive character. It has! It is orthodox and that's the end of it, although I never told the school it was so and I don't believe one of our pupils knows what 'orthodox' means. We mean to teach the precepts of Jesus Christ, accepting them as inspired and as recorded in the Bible.[2]**

The college received financial backing primarily from the theologically liberal American Missionary Association and Unitarians. Although Hampton (Institute) University now provides a wonderful liberal arts education, evangelicals missed a monumental opportunity to support the school in the late 1800's when it held an evangelical standard in its charter.

Imagine the impact that Hampton University would have made on Hampton Roads and the world if it had graduated generations of conservative evangelical black leaders equipped there for the purpose of local and world evangelization. Segregation prevented its partnership with most evangelical churches, Bible colleges and seminaries that remained closed to blacks until years after the **Brown versus Board of Education** Supreme Court decision. White liberals deserve much of the credit for providing funding during this era for black colleges, like Hampton University, across the South.

During the horrors of the Jim Crow years, evangelicals treated black theologians like children who could not keep themselves from the earthly attractions of the liberal theologians' social gospel. Instead of seizing the opportunity to use the Bible to bring racial and economic justice to African-Americans, evangelicals segregated themselves on both sides of the Mason-Dixon Line.

Christians' silence during this oppressive era enabled the terrors of lynchings to go unchallenged. In her autobiography, Ida B. Wells (1862-1931), a Christian African-American crusader against lynchings and other oppressions, reports how evangelical leaders, like Dwight L. Moody, ignored lynching atrocities to placate whites:

> **Christian bodies and moral associations do not touch the question. It is the easiest way to get along in the South (and those places in the North where lynchings take place) to ignore the question altogether; our American Christians are too busy saving the souls of white Christians from burning in hell fire to save the lives of black ones**

from present burning in fires kindled by white Christians. The feelings of the people who commit these acts must not be hurt by protesting against this sort of thing, and so the bodies of the victims of mob hate must be sacrificed, and the country disgraced because of that fear to speak out.[3]

Neglect like this by white Christian leaders eventually caused the true gospel of Jesus Christ to become discredited as white doctrine by many black leaders.

Their loss of faith in the biblical Gospel and the spiritual devastation this produced only became worse in the Civil Rights Movement in the 1960's when white evangelicals remained silent. While whites, including so-called Christians, beat and imprisoned blacks during Martin Luther King's passive resistance, King felt abandoned and betrayed by white Christians, especially by evangelicals.

This racist neglect still cripples the witness of white Christians in the inner city and in many third world countries. Ironically, the cruelty endured by African-Americans now opens doors for black missionaries in countries that suffered the same racial oppression.

Some evangelical Christians might take pride in the history of northern white believers' participation in the abolitionist movement. Our celebration of their commitment becomes tempered by the realization that most of their stands for justice did not include racial integration and that they promoted liberal doctrine among African-Americans. The injustices resulting from continued segregation in the North grew with the migration of African-Americans to its cities.

The racial division in northern Christian denominations, the moving of northern black theologians toward liberalism, and an increase in black rioting and militancy in the North reflected the failure of northern white evangelical Christians to bring justice to their own communities during the abolition movement. Southern whites had pointed out, before the Civil War, prevalent injustices by whites in the North against immigrants and declared that abolitionists' arguments against slavery amounted to hypocrisy.[4]

Satan still uses segregation injustices to strengthen this foothold today. White churches that find themselves in racially changing neighborhoods become especially susceptible. They may invite blacks, or other persons of color, to their services but often do not "feel that their people are ready" to submit to black church leadership.

In other words, they welcome blacks to worship and to participate in programs but they will not allow a black pastor, elder, or deacon to govern them. Because they refuse to accept black people as potential leaders, they are unwilling to disciple and equip them for church offices. Some may go as far to appoint a token black deacon but this also smacks of injustice and only worsens a church's relationship with its neighbors.

Our Lord justly intended that shepherds in His church qualify through calling, character and spiritual gifts, not on the basis of race. Blacks, whites, and persons of all races in the local body of Christ should witness racial diversity in their servant leadership. Their children should see diverse adult role models submitting to one another's gifts. I believe that this practical demonstration of humility and reconciliation in the church will have a transforming effect in the community.

White churches, ministries and educational institutions

seeking to increase participation of African-Americans must take seriously their needs for the support, role modeling and fellowship of black leadership. Living in a racialized society creates identity crises for blacks (and whites), which is compounded for Christians by the divides between the races over good doctrine.

I agree with Beverly Tatum who describes a cycle of racial identity development that African-Americans undergo from adolescence through adulthood. She explains how in a racist society blacks need the understanding and support of other blacks who have overcome the same hurts and obstacles. They not only hunger for Afro-centric relevant information, they also seek opportunities to help their children develop healthy racial identities through interactions with other African-American children.[5]

Black churches meet these identity needs for many, which explains the racial divide in evangelical Christianity. Blacks attending white-governed evangelical churches lose the benefit of having black leadership when dealing with racism in and outside of the church walls.   They also lose having role models for their children.

Just as having all white teachers in school conveys to black children that excellence in education is a white trait, having all white spiritual leadership subtly communicates to black children that they are spiritually inferior as a race. As I said in the last chapter, add to these losses the phenomenon that many black theologians in the late 1960's used liberalism as the theological framework for linking black identity development to doctrines that deny the essentials of evangelical beliefs. As a result, to develop strong racial identities, many African-American leaders attended, and still attend, seminaries that rejected true evangelical doctrine.

To end the racial divide in evangelical Christianity, we must appreciate the difficulties that African-Americans face when embracing evangelical doctrine. During the 1960's and 70's, some African-Americans broke through racist barriers to receive evangelical biblical training, to attend white evangelical churches or to send their children to white Christian schools.

They not only heroically endured racial discrimination from white evangelicals, they also endured the hurtful stigma of being isolated by liberal black church leaders who labeled them "Uncle Toms," "orioes," and "tokens" for crossing white racial and doctrinal divides. This double separation - race and doctrine - between black and white Christians alienated blacks from evangelicals and created a void in black evangelical leadership that remains today.

Evangelical Christians must remove institutional barriers that prevent the training and empowering of black evangelical leaders. I emphasized in my "DNA Analysis" in Chapter 2 that nostalgia is one such barrier difficult for many older white Christians to overcome. I have observed that those who attend segregated churches in neighborhoods that have become racially diverse often try to preserve their pasts. Though the neighborhoods have changed, they refuse to change their attitudes about maintaining segregated church leadership.

Amazed that few blacks attend churches governed only by white people, members of these churches often blame the problem on the style of music that is played in worship services. They may refuse to racially integrate to preserve their worship style or they might spend a lot of energy trying to adapt their music to attract blacks, without realizing that their racism is the root of the offense.

White churches seeking to evangelize their unchurched

black neighbors have several options for developing black evangelical leadership. These strategies include aggressively pursuing the limited number of biblically trained black evangelical leaders, recruiting and providing seminary training to the present generation of Christian black college students or evangelizing, equipping and empowering unchurched African-Americans.

For effective leadership development, evangelical Christians must understand how segregation contributed to the doctrinal divide between black and white Christians. We must correct how this divide still hinders the mobilization of leaders for the spiritual harvest.

Segregation Inventory

1. What is the history of racial segregation in your ministry and city?

2. How has racial segregation impacted the doctrine of local churches in your city?

3. What initiatives has your ministry taken in the past five years to end the racial divide between blacks and whites?

4. Action Step: Analyze your own environment and make lists of factors that perpetuate or prevent racial segregation.

10 | Divided Doctrine

The conservatives who say, "Let us not move so fast," and the extremists who say, "Let us go out and whip the world," would tell you that they are as far apart as the poles. But there is one striking parallel: They accomplish nothing; for they do not reach the people who have a crying need to be free. Dr. Martin Luther King, Jr. [1]

I get an eerie feeling of doom when watching entire communities of young men live in a state of bitter hopelessness. As a basketball coach, I often see gymnasiums filled with these men. I see teenagers who remain academically ineligible for high school sports every year. The pipelines of community sports teams that feed these athletes to their high schools are broken because these students cannot participate due to academic failure.

During neighborhood basketball games these youth vent their anger toward the authorities and each other. They curse to communicate the frustration in their hearts. Many end up incarcerated. As teenagers many have children themselves and recycle their hurt. These young men represent the future of their neighborhoods.

In this spiritual harvest, we must understand how the history, doctrine and politics of false teachers have funneled down to the young theologians in inner city gangs. This foothold of false teaching has exploded into a street theology that provides them justification for violent lawlessness.

These men grab onto the bitterness of black militant groups and mix it with their own hurts, hopelessness and isolation. "Any means necessary" becomes more than rhetoric. They throw off the laws of white government and suspect white conspiracies behind every political and religious corner. They view engaging in the business of illegal drugs, which they sell in their neighborhoods, as a necessary means of survival. They believe white government officials somehow get a cut of the drug profits. In their opinion, the police and criminal justice systems work for the benefit of white oppressors.

Many of these young men govern and empower themselves by deadly force. No one strolls through their neighborhoods without their permission. No one represents them in religion or politics. They develop their own little worlds and systems within the confines of ghettoized neighborhoods. Many view most white believers as oppressive hypocrites and assume that the Christianity in their communities is just for old people, sissies or shysters. A fearless inventory of American history traces their beliefs back to the devastating consequences of white theologians who distorted the Word of God.

When black and white Christians study the Scriptures together in honest relationships of trust, we can counter this theology of the streets. Our demonstrations of racial reconciliation and sacrificial service break through the Evil One's deceptions about the Bible and about Christians, as the Holy Spirit draws inner city men into the studies.

We call this kind of outreach "bulldog evangelism"

where we grab onto these men and refuse to let go! Intervention comes through the miraculous power of the Holy Spirit. It happens in their homes and in their neighborhoods. The truth sets men free. We make truth known by prayerfully coming together as one spiritual race of believers who live out God's Word in the community of God's grace.

Unfortunately, many evangelicals, who are supposed to value "rightly dividing the Word of truth," have allowed God's Word to be wrongly divided along racial lines for centuries. Scripture, manipulated through the lens of racial superiority, became proof texts by which evangelical believers "justified" their horrible acts of injustice, including their domination and economic evangelism.

This false teaching allowed, and still allows, the Evil One to discredit the truth of all scripture, especially Christ's Gospel. Bogus interpretations of the curse on Canaan in Genesis, slavery in I Corinthians 7:21 and the predestination of blacks to be subservient to whites fueled the racism behind slavery and segregation's injustices.

Does Satan still have a foothold through this false teaching today? I say emphatically -"Yes!" This racist heresy alienated, and still alienates, many theologians and religious leaders of African descent by tempting them to devalue and/or reject the **authority** and **infallibility** of the Word of God.

Segregation in Biblical training seems horrible today, but only a few decades ago key evangelical Bible colleges and seminaries refused to integrate. The hurt and loss of goodwill toward these institutions generated by this one policy continues to diminish the spiritual impact of these institutions to this day. These institutions have the unenviable task of recruiting black students whose grandfathers were barred from their campuses in the 1950's.

Our evangelical institutions and scholars remain silent about this history. They quietly recruit black students and faculty to change the tide of black opinion gradually.

Why not openly admit our theological guilt and cry out for justice in and through true doctrine? White Bible scholars should tackle this issue because they can openly repent for generations of white theologians who maligned or disobeyed the Word of Christ. Let us get our dirty laundry out in the open so we may ask for forgiveness and take on new robes of righteousness through repentance.

Then, by demonstrating that we have been corrected, our scholars may, like Apollos in Acts 18:25 and 28, speak with great fervor and teach accurately about Jesus, vigorously debating and proving from the Scriptures that Jesus is the Christ. Let our white scholars publish their repentance and then join black evangelicals in powerfully defending our faith.

With understanding, these scholars could help our missions boards and churches realize the offense we perpetuate by sending out wave after wave of white missionaries into countries and communities already alienated from God's Word by white oppression.

Our Bible colleges could help open the eyes of the next generation of spiritual leaders by trumpeting justice and mercy as truths fundamental to the Christian faith. For the first time they may come to value a reconciled witness for Christ.

What better way to disarm the Evil One and powerfully, clearly and boldly proclaim the good news of Jesus Christ, than for black and white Christians to lock hearts and hands in the harvest field at home and abroad?

Oppressive racism by whites in the South and North

gave Satan the foothold to divide theologians on good doctrine. Through white theologians, the Evil One effectively separated the doctrines of biblical authority from the doctrines of justice and mercy, as well as the doctrine of the supernatural intervention of the Holy Spirit.

Through the continual racialization of such doctrines in the fundamentalist, liberal and **Pentecostal** movements, he maligns the Word of God, discredits the Gospel and sends a host of false teachers into the inner city to prey on those lost in the confusion.

Enough time has passed for evangelicals to sort out good from bad doctrines and understand how to equip workers for the harvest. We must comprehend the reasons why many persons of African descent equate orthodox Christianity with white oppression, while they associate the heretical doctrines of liberalism with justice and freedom.

Unlike Neo-orthodoxy, which seeks to merge the best in both liberal and evangelical doctrines, we must defend all the essential doctrines of the faith while wholeheartedly obeying the literal commands of Christ about mercy and justice. If combining these teachings crosses doctrinal divides from the past, then we must let the Word of God's authority dictate our response. We must cross the divide that separates evangelical doctrine from good doctrine that calls for Christ's followers to act justly and love mercy.

Evangelicals must cherish the good doctrines of justice and mercy regardless of how liberal theologians have used them to reject the Gospel. Jesus exalted justice and mercy as the foundation of His purposes for our lives. Evangelicals must obey the commands of Christ to learn and practice these priorities.

Justice and mercy have been the chief tenants of white

liberalism for so long that evangelicals have abandoned them as misguided attempts to earn salvation. Even so, by pursuing justice and mercy liberals have accomplished much good. Believing in their ability to bring society into the Kingdom of God, they have worked to improve education, health care and living conditions among the poor. They addressed racism and segregation. They also confronted evangelical hypocrisy.

Now evangelicals must repent and embrace our biblical mandate to love justice and show mercy, not because we seek to usher in the Kingdom of God, but because we seek to obey the King.

The Gospel and Social Activism

Satan polarized the teaching of Christ between fundamentalists and liberals with devastating effects on the evangelical witness in our inner cities. Fundamentalists, entrenched in the battle for the Bible, opposed anything embraced by liberalism. They rejected mercy and justice as priorities for accomplishing the purposes of God because liberals emphasized them in their social gospel. Christ's teachings became torn apart in the debate. Liberals championed justice on earth and evangelicals focused on salvation in heaven.

Although both white evangelicals and liberals practiced segregation after the Civil War, liberals accepted blacks into their seminaries and anchored the abolitionist movement. As I previously described, these abolitionists, motivated by Christ's teaching on justice and mercy, established black colleges and seminaries after the Civil War under the doctrinal tenants of theologically liberal Congregationalist and Unitarian's social outreach ministries.

The inner cities lost a connection to the saving Gospel of

Jesus Christ when fundamentalists stopped doing good in a reaction to liberals' social action.

Because these liberals had lived out Christ's commands for justice and mercy during Reconstruction while denying His Gospel, many black theologians adopted their liberal presuppositions about the authority of Scripture. Deep hurt and bitterness from the injustices of slavery, cruel oppression during Jim Crow, political disenfranchisement, and a distorted self-image from white degradation fueled the Black Power Movement with its call for liberation and self-reliance.

White liberals' philosophical idealism, inclusion of other world religions, attacks on the Bible and acceptance of evolution made black power transferable to religion. Liberalism gave black theologians the framework for rejecting the authority of Scripture and Jesus' Gospel as white doctrine.

As a result, many African-Americans worshipping in traditional black denominations trusted in their good works for salvation instead of Christ's atonement on the cross. Many still believe that loving God and helping their fellow man will get them to heaven, even though most lay persons accept the Bible as the Word of God. Satan achieved His goal of hiding the truth about the born-again experience.

When liberals funded the establishment of these black colleges during the Reconstruction period, they also laid the doctrinal foundation for black theologians to reject the authority of Scripture and to elevate **Black Experience** into its place. Blacks graduating from prominent northern, predominantly white liberal seminaries - while most evangelical institutions remained segregated - compounded the advancement of liberal doctrine among blacks.

The acceptance of white theories of reason and evolution by blacks made the creation of new theologies reasonable. They began to see their doctrine as an evolving divine and dynamic process centered on their struggle for freedom from white domination. **Black Power** provided the impetus for a new black gospel and the resulting **Black Theology** Movement of the 1960's. African-American theologians founded their teachings on presuppositions about the Bible taken from white liberal doctrine and evolution.

Presently, only thirty-five percent of black pastors in the U.S. hold a world view that embraces the accuracy of Biblical teaching, the omnipotence and omniscience of God, salvation by grace alone and personal responsibility to evangelize.[2]

Cone uses Dr. Martin Luther King Jr.'s writings, for example, to indicate that white liberal theologians influenced King to reject evangelical doctrine. According to Cone, King had rejected "everything that the fundamentalist and orthodox theologians were affirming as essentials of the faith: the inerrancy of the Bible, virgin birth of Jesus, substitutionary [. . .] atonement, bodily resurrection of Jesus, miracles and similar creedal formulations."[3] Cone also reports that King learned George Fredrick Hegel's ideas from white liberals, who used the theory of evolution to interpret history. Karl Marx used this same kind of reasoning to argue that civilizations evolve from capitalism to the higher stage of communism.[4]

Those adopting liberalism's assumptions about the Bible to create Black Theology also risk inheriting its problems. Liberal churches have been steadily declining in membership for seventy years because, in denying the authority of the Scriptures, they forfeited their means to inspire commitment for the spiritual harvest. Liberal theology generated members who believe that the Lord of the harvest is dead and His Word is untrustworthy and erroneous.

Left with social institutions, potential churchgoers calculate that the benefits of participating in liberal churches are not worth the energy, time and money.[5] Both white and black liberals have lost the means to create the fervor, spiritual life and power in members needed for making sacrifices and taking risks to intervene in our inner cities.

According to the Journal of Religion and Public Life, in 1993 the single best predictor of church participation was orthodox Christian belief, and the teaching that the only way of salvation is through faith in Jesus Christ.[6] I believe this predictor holds true today for traditional African-American churches. If they deny His resurrection power and Great Commission, they face the same demise as the declining number of back yard gardens that I talked about in this book's preface. Without a legacy of workers for the spiritual harvest, their congregations risk becoming extinct when their memories of past glories fade away. Many church buildings in urban areas already just exist for commuters from the suburbs and remain disconnected from the poor.

In contrast, more and more black believers today, unimpressed with white intellectualism, are forming a new theologically conservative movement. They embrace the freedom to determine where to place the authority of their beliefs without dependence upon white doctrinal influences. They find this liberation by letting the Bible speak for itself through careful study and by taking the life, commands, and Gospel of Jesus Christ at face value.

This new movement, free from white racist teachings and from white liberalism's presuppositions, empowers persons of African descent to spiritually intervene in the inner city and throughout the world. This is a positive spiritual revolution, which grows today in spite of theological rhetoric. With appreciation and study of the Scriptures, these black theologians accept the doctrinal essentials of the evangelical faith that Satan once hid inside the segregated walls of white racialized fundamentalism. This is a cause for rejoicing as the light of God's truth is finally beginning to shine forth and is uniting faith in the true Gospel with acting justly and showing mercy!

Now African-Americans are able to love justice and mercy without becoming doctrinally liberal and may embrace the literal interpretation of the Bible without becoming racist fundamentalists. They may choose truth and disarm the Evil One's attempts to divide good doctrine between opposing racialized theologies. This movement inspires obedience to the living Lord and elevates blacks to take their rightful place as leaders in His international harvest.

Tom Skinner pulled no punches on this debate by concluding at Urbana 70:

> **There is no possible way you can talk about preaching the gospel if you do not want to deal with the issues that bind people. If your gospel is an "either-or" gospel, I must reject it. Any gospel that does not talk about delivering to man a personal Savior who will free him from the personal bondage of sin and grant him eternal life and does not at the same time speak to the issue of enslavement, the issue of injustice, the issue of inequality - any gospel that does not want to go where people are hungry and poverty-stricken and set them free in the name of Jesus Christ is not the gospel.**[7]

Ironies of Secular Humanism

Calling Christians to act justly and love mercy through social action is quite complicated by the ironies associated with combining theological issues with secular politics. The doctrinal debate about the social gospel between liberal and evangelical theologians is inseparably interwoven with the opposing political party platforms of secular humanists and conservatives.

Francis Schaeffer in *A Christian Manifesto* even warns that liberal theology is just secular humanism expressed in theological terms. He asserts that liberal theology and the secular humanism behind liberal politics are both part of the same threat to the Christian faith.

He mixes theology and politics when he blames Christian educators, theologians, and lawyers for failing in their responsibility to sound the warning trumpet against the world's shift toward humanism. He challenges evangelicals to do better by "stop being experts in only seeing these things in bits and pieces." Schaeffer calls for seeing as a whole the humanistic worldview behind the advancement of evolution, liberal theology, and arbitrary situational sociological law. He warns that humanistic court rulings will result in the loss of faith and freedom and he calls for civil disobedience to prevent authoritarianism in government courts.[8]

During our nation's recent history most white evangelicals avoided social causes, remained silent during segregation and the civil rights movement, took a strong stand against secular humanism, and then became a conservative political force within the Republican Party. When they finally found their moral voice to speak up against injustices they found themselves on the other side of the political fence from African-American Christians who have the same moral values. How ironic that Satan's foothold of divided doctrine about social action successfully separated White and Black Christians along political party lines. With this and many other ironic divisions, I believe Satan diabolically prevented Black and White Christians from standing together on theological and political issues.

Martin Luther King, Jr. alluded to some of this irony when he wrote, "I would be the last to condemn the thousands of sincere and dedicated people outside of churches who have labored unselfishly through various humanitarian movements to cure the world of social evils, for I would rather a man be a committed humanist than an uncommitted Christian."[9]

Consider the following startling ironies between African-Americans and evangelical whites brought on during this onslaught of humanism. These ironies boomerang back on our nation today and destroy faith, freedom and the value of life in the inner cities:

Irony of Social Neglect. As most evangelicals remained silent during the oppression of blacks during slavery and in the Jim Crow era, many liberal theologians and secular (atheist) humanists showed mercy to persons of African descent.

Irony of Doctrinal Demise. The silence of evangelical theologians and lawyers contributed to the advancement of liberalism/humanism in America. Then liberal theologians and politicians provided African-Americans the groundwork for creating a Black Theology, which is both theologically and politically liberal. Ironically, evangelicals' neglect during this time period destroyed the faith of many African-American theologians in the literal interpretation and absolute authority of the Bible.

Irony of Human Rights. A move towards winning black civil rights was imbedded in the humanistic worldview shift that Schaeffer called evangelicals to reject.

Irony of Political Action. The liberal (by majority) Supreme Court ruled against separate-but-equal segregation laws and thereby forced racial integrations in schools (1954) and in transportation facilities (1962) upon many whites who had been violently discriminating against blacks. In 1973 the liberal Supreme Court forced violent abortion rights upon our nation using the humanistic sociological law that Schaeffer had called Christians to protest against.

Then around 1990 pro-life evangelicals wanting to follow the pattern of black civil disobedience failed to stop abortion because black Christians having the political clout to end it endorsed the pro-abortion Democratic Party instead. The vast majority of African-Americans, following the pattern set by white believers during past injustices against blacks, remained silent about abortion.

Let me repeat this irony for emphasis because it continues to this day. Like whites who remained silent and neglected fighting for the rights of blacks during slavery, Jim Crow and the Civil Rights Movement, black Christians now remain silent and neglect the rights of their unborn while the horrible injustice of abortion prevails. White pro-life leaders have not been able to convince African-Americans to demonstrate against abortion even though the number of black babies murdered by abortionists disproportionately increases.

Irony of a Reconciliation Attempt. Black and white men at Promise Keepers committed themselves to racial reconciliation in the late 1990's. According to sociologists Michael Emerson and Christian Smith these men subsequently fell short on this promise and ghettoized their leader, which sustained status quo racial divides among them.[10] Liberal religious and secular leaders criticized Promise Keepers for making shallow attempts to bring this reconciliation by saying that these men failed to commit to overcoming the institutionalized racism that maintains the segregation of their ancestors.[11]

Irony of Debate on Moral Values. Evangelicals took a stand with their vote in the 2004 election against humanism's moral decline. Ironically, the majority of African American voters, most having the same moral convictions as these "Red State" Christians, backed candidates who ran on pro-abortion and gay marriage platforms because these politicians promised economic justice for the poor.

In addition, five million African-Americans in the U.S. currently attend churches where their leaders preach, and often broadcast, **neo-Pentecostal** teachings about speaking into existence miracles of healing and prosperity. Most of these same people also keep silent on abortion, which ironically kills more African-Americans than cancer, heart disease and all homicides combined.[12]

The Gospel and Political Activism

In recent years a new divide has surfaced as some evangelical leaders began questioning the value of Christian political activism for reversing the nation's moral deterioration. This introspection generated controversy among evangelical that needs to be resolved to prevent Satan from getting another foothold to undermine the Gospel's impact in the inner city. Unlike the "either-or" social gospel debate that had pitted evangelicals against liberals on social issues, the more recent disagreement occurred among evangelicals themselves regarding the Gospel and political activism.

John MacArthur and James Dobson led the two sides of the debate about whether Christians should focus their resources on preaching the gospel (MacArthur) versus investing in political lobbying and protests (Dobson) to end society's moral decline.[13]

I spend myself for the proclamation of the Gospel in agreement with MacArthur's priorities. Without doubt, I concur with him that Christian activists like James Dobson of Focus on the Family ought to uncompromisingly proclaim the Gospel to bring repentance from sin. John MacArthur and Cal Thomas questioned whether Dobson has neglected the proclamation of the Gospel by compromising his witness to pursue political influence as a means to save America.

In response, Tom Minnery, Vice-President of Public Policy for Focus on the Family published the book *Why You Can't Stay Silent* to present biblical and historical arguments for Christian activism. He also used Jesus' Good Samaritan parable to demonstrate God's call for compassion and justice.[14]

Touching issues related to the inner city harvest, Minnery chooses the founders of an abolitionist movement, the Salvation Army and the protests by black Christians during their Civil Rights Movement to support his arguments that Christians should engage in political action.[15] From the perspective of the inner city harvest and judging from the spiritual outcomes of all of these movements, these examples could also support MacArthur's accusation that political activism dilutes the Gospel. For all the billions of dollars Christians have invested in social and political activism during the last century, we have yet to evangelize the inner city. Ironically, many of the abolitionists' resources also advanced liberal theology, which laid the doctrinal foundation for Black Theology's rejection of the Gospel.

In addition, mercy and justice causes for the inner city poor do not appear next to Minnery's pro-life arguments, which gives liberals more good reasons to denounce evangelical motives. Given the way Satan has politically and doctrinally polarized most whites and blacks, this lack of emphasis on the plight of the inner poor may undermine the desired political results of activism.

From the inner city's viewpoint both camps have credibility problems to overcome, especially when they attempt to stand alone for God without the full witness and support of the entire Body of Christ.

One the one hand, politics cannot save without the Gospel's transforming power. For example, the much needed welfare reform that Christians supported also created economic pressure on impoverished mothers to use abortion as birth control. I have observed in Norfolk over the last fifteen years of welfare reform the loss of pro-life values among many of the poor. On the other hand, Christians with MacArthur's convictions about evangelism have already compromised the Gospel for five hundred years through racism and segregation.

Nevertheless, combining these causes makes a more powerful witness for Christ. Dobson already blesses the inner city by confronting many of the prominent political and cultural forces that promote Christian moral compromise. Today's Christian political activists provide believers the knowledge, support base and conviction to take a stand for righteousness in the face of government or cultural opposition, which ultimately also blesses inner city families.

Minnery concludes correctly that those who proclaim the Gospel find themselves asking, "What does righteousness command?"[16] Risking controversy and persecution that may alienate some unbelievers, the inner city harvesters must take unpopular stands that make them activists.

He misses the chance to support his call for Christian activism by showing how evangelical silence and neglect in the face of immoral government and cultural pressures resulted in devastating spiritual consequences during slavery, Jim Crow and the civil rights movement. He could have made an argument for activism by reporting how southern Bible colleges chose to remain segregated in the fifties during a time when their state governments affirmed white supremacy.

These Bible colleges held the evangelical position of their day that Christians should not push for social and political change. Their board members compromised and kept them segregated for almost a decade past the Brown versus Board of Education Supreme Court decision. Unjust political and cultural influences of that time prevailed, while schools emphasized the preaching of the Gospel, with devastating spiritual consequences that remain today.

The absence of Dobson-like activism left those in their faculty, students and alumni who sought righteousness to work within the segregated framework to attempt racial justice.[17] As a result, by not speaking out to defend civil liberties and to change cultural injustices, white evangelicals offended oppressed African-Americans and maligned the true Gospel.

Evangelicals' failure to stand against past injustices shows why James Dobson is needed to mobilize evangelicals for the inner city and to heighten their commitment to protect the religious freedom that allows the Gospel to be openly proclaimed there. He also prepares Christians for the inner city harvest by challenging them to make a difference in our nation. I have found that most politically involved Christians openly champion inner city evangelism. They seem to be the first to recognize the limitations of activism and the need for the transforming Gospel to make lasting changes in our communities.

Another positive aspect about Dobson is that he also strongly influences middle class evangelical women who often become the first to connect with inner city families. Their compassion drives them to seek ways to make a difference among the poor and to mobilize their churches to do the same. These women are usually early innovators who recruit husbands and church leaders for inner city outreaches.

Since MacArthur and Dobson's points of view call for the end of evangelical silence and each of their causes is vitally important to the inner city harvest, their ministries could sharpen each other and more comprehensively impact the inner city. By bringing together the untapped potentials of evangelism and activism, evangelical leaders may challenge silent Christians to speak up and mobilize for the neglected inner city harvest. Their preaching and teaching radio ministries could also provide platforms to confront evangelical structures that sustain racial division within the Church.

Instead of making the harvest a **zero-sum game**, which would assume that Christian resources are so limited that we must choose between evangelism and activism, the LORD promises grace for accomplishing His priorities of mercy and justice while we proclaim the Gospel:

And if you spend yourself in behalf of the hungry and satisfy the needs of the oppressed, then your light will shine in the darkness, and your night will become like the noonday. The LORD will guide you always; He will satisfy your needs in a sun-scortched land and will strengthen your frame. You will be like a well-watered garden, like a spring whose waters never fail . . . you will be called Repairer of Broken Walls, Restorer of Streets and Dwellings (Isaiah 58:10-12 NIV).

Sociologist Robert Franklin identifies five categories for describing the theological and political orientation of black churches related to social issues. This typology may be helpful for understanding ways that most evangelical churches view outreach to the poor, since socio-economic factors may now define the categories better than race or doctrine.[18]

Franklin identifies "***grassroots revivalists***" as churches that focus on individual responsibility, personal salvation and personal morality. This category represents the views of most white evangelical congregations. Their theology of personal salvation may provide the rational for disengaging themselves from taking political action. They take John MacArthur's position that our nation's moral decline can only be stopped by God changing the hearts of people through the Gospel.

"***Pragmatic accommadationists***" want to make the existing political and economic systems work for those not benefiting from them and they avoid protest and confrontations. Most white, black and multi-racial churches fall in this category. Congregations in this second category may also fit in the first.

"***Redemptive nationalists***" are congregations that strategically participate in the political system to advance their own interests without obligating themselves to secular authorities. This type may apply to evangelical churches that form non-profits and use government funding in faith-based initiatives.

"*Positive thought materialists*" emphasize individual prosperity through God's provision of success, wealth and health. These are the "words of faith" type churches and they seek ways to use political and economic systems to support individual interests rather than community empowerment.

"*Prophetic radicals*" devote themselves to social justice. Based on a liberal perspective, they call for sacrificial action to radically change individual hearts and social institutions. As the black middle class grows, the number of black churches in this category declines as fewer emphasize social justice. A 2000 study of black churches in Indianapolis found no black churches in this prophetic category.[19]

When Jesus commands us to show mercy like the Samaritan did in Luke 10, He gives us the commission to proclaim the Gospel of individual salvation through our devotion to justice. Our personal sacrifices to change both individual hearts and social institutions must exceed the waning commitment of prophetic radicals.

Just as Jesus confronted the systemic injustices in the Pharisaical program, our moral inventory must tear down unjust strongholds within evangelical thinking. From there we might reclaim the credibility to confront social injustices in our society and world. Although millions of evangelicals have sought personal justice for a long time, institutional injustices still hinder the inner city harvest.

Most evangelicals still ghettoize the poor in my opinion. We do this in the following ways:

1. We let fear immobilize us.
2. We fail to evangelize our inner cities.
3. We emphasize programs rather relationship-based evangelism.
4. We abandon impoverished children in public schools.
5. We do not make evangelical Biblical training available in the inner city.
6. We do not mobilize African-Americans for world missions.
7. Most of our churches remain racially divided.
8. Many evangelical leaders leave out justice and mercy from the purposes of God.

Because something is wrong in our system, we fail to obey Christ's Great Commission in the inner cities.

Surely Jesus calls us to be more than accommadationists. Yet, as evangelicals continue to neglect the spiritual harvest in the inner city, social injustices go unchallenged. Consider these current statistics in the U.S.: an average of 1,452 black babies die by abortions every day,[20] one-third of black men between the ages of 19 and 29 are in the legal system's jails, prisons or probation services. One-half of the two million people in America's prisons are black.[21]

These statistics reflect the tragic consequences of neglect. Evangelicals who believe that the Gospel, received on an individual bases, is powerful enough to change these statistics must sacrificially mobilize in the inner city to intervene early and comprehensively. In addition, evangelicals must also accept their responsibility as citizens of a democratic society and use their political clout to act justice and show mercy.

By pragmatically working within the system, we fail to challenge systemic evangelical and social problems. By default we promote the status quo, undermine just action and prevent the fulfillment of God's priority purposes. I will explain in later chapters how accomplishing God's purposes with mercy and just action will bless both the individual and the community.

The Gospel and Pentecostalism

One would think that Pentecostal, Charismatic and mainline conservative Christians would blend together into a unified evangelical witness to the inner city. Persons entering the inner city harvest need to be prepared for the doctrinal disagreements between these branches of evangelicalism and understand how each has their own set of issues related to the inner city.

As most readers probably know, the Pentecostal movement in this country began at the turn of the 20th Century in what is commonly known as the Azusa Street Revival. Racism that existed in the start of this movement added another dimension to the doctrinal divide in the inner city harvest. The white Assemblies of God and the black Church of God in Christ denominations grew out of a racial split of the Azusa Mission around 1900. An African-American student, William J. Seymour, attended a white segregated Bible school by sitting outside the open door of his teacher, Charles Fox Parham.

Later, Seymour started the Azusa Mission as an interracial Pentecostal church, characterized by the first practice of speaking in unknown tongues as a sign from God. Parham denounced this revival because he concluded that the unorthodox worship behavior of the racially diverse congregation had become degrading. The church divided in a racial split, which spawned the two largest current Pentecostal denominations in the world. The Assemblies of God grew out of Parham's white faction. The remaining black followers of Seymour became associated with Henry T. Mason and became the largest black denomination, the Church of God in Christ.

Coming from the Holiness movement and then networking with African-American denominations, black Pentecostal churches may align today anywhere on the evangelical/liberal theological continuum. The Church of God in Christ denomination's doctrinal statement affirms the authority of Scripture and its literal interpretation.[22] Some black Pentecostals also embrace the social gospel and elevate the authority of Black Experience, aligning more with Black Theology.

Black Pentecostals provide the spiritual harvest in the inner city with at least three important dynamics. They expect the Spirit of God to miraculously intervene in supernatural ways including giving victory in spiritual warfare, healing and provision. For a second dynamic, their expectation of God's power strengthens their resolve to minister in the worst environments to those in the worst bondage. Black Pentecostals also use radio and television well to connect with unchurched people.

Non-Pentecostal evangelicals may miss appreciating these dynamics because at least four characteristics of Black Pentecostalism divide them. First, black Pentecostals' church government and hierarchy of bishops resemble Roman Catholic authoritarian rule and politics.[23] Black Pentecostal pastors carry the same kind of autocratic authority in their churches.

Second, pastors support their centralized authority with testimonies of receiving direct revelation from God for their sermons and to govern their churches. Many non-Pentecostal evangelical theologians believe that Pentecostals undermine the authority of Scripture when claiming to receive direct revelation from God through experiences.[24]

Third, non-Pentecostal evangelicals do not accept black Pentecostals' traditional ways of giving persons the Holy Spirit during conversions, during spiritual baptisms and during subsequent fillings by the Spirit.

The fourth divide centers on Biblical scholarship, which black Pentecostals may value less than non-Pentecostal evangelicals because they emphasize receiving direct revelation and because they may have weaker educational backgrounds. These four differences add up to create a significant divide between non-Pentecostal evangelicals and black Pentecostals.

The racial divide between white and black Pentecostals also hurts their witness. "Seymour came to believe that blacks and whites worshiping together was a surer sign of God's blessing and the Spirit's healing presence than speaking in tongues. The fact that the church had nationally split along racial lines meant that the charismatic ideal of cooperation with the Spirit had been foiled by the forces of racism." [25]

An estimated one-third of mainline black denominational churches have embraced neo-Pentecostal (meaning Charismatic) theology. They have adopted worship styles, structures and emphases that resemble white charismatic churches. Neo-Pentecostal churches focus on reaching individuals over social action, attracting the black middle class, forming megachurches, establishing non-profit social outreaches and promoting prosperity theology.[26]

Black ministers from traditional churches have criticized black neo-Pentecostal leaders for forsaking social action and its justice and mercy causes. Having adopted the styles and structures of white Christians, black neo-Pentecostals must be careful

to strategically engage their inner city neighbors and avoid repli-
cating white silent neglect. Strategic planning for them is vitally
important because their prosperity theology encourages "black
flight" from the inner city and reinforces the survival mentality
that I explained in Chapter 3. Neo-Pentecostals must especially
avoid recycling white church structures and cultures that have
design, neighborliness and action levels ("DNA") that disengage
them from the inner city.

Since this book challenges Christian schools to include
inner city families in their missions, I repeat this appeal here to
the predominantly black middle-class neo-Pentecostal megachurches and the predominantly white middle-class churches or
groups that establish separate Christian schools in the same
cities. If combining their schools is not possible, are there ways
they could strategically partner together or pool resources to
enroll the inner city poor?

I pose three questions about racial division for leaders of
these schools to consider:

1. Are their racially-divided independent schools
   inadvertently creating separate-but-equal scenarios
   that segregationists would have loved and have
   fought for in the past?

2. Are their separate white and black evangelical
   schools accomplishing in private education what
   racist people had hoped to sustain in public school
   segregation?

3. Do their schools consciously avoid making private
   school education a way for parents to sidestep the
   1954 Brown versus Board of Education Supreme
   Court decision that forced integration of public
   schools?

A Prayer for Laborers

Lord of the harvest we look to you to thrust forth laborers into the inner city who excel in applying sound doctrine.

Send workers whose level of commitment to justice and mercy exceeds that of liberalism. May they spend themselves for the empowerment of inner city men and women and tirelessly serve to bring an end to the racial divide there and to break the cycle of poverty.

Send workers whose commitment to the intervening power of the Holy Spirit exceeds that of Pentecostalism. May they powerfully break down spiritual strongholds, expect the Holy Spirit's anointing and miraculous intervention, supernaturally minister in His gifts to the least of these and faithfully praise the Lord regardless of economic or educational circumstances.

Provide laborers whose commitment to the Word of God exceeds that of fundamentalism. May they stand firm in the inner city, studying and proclaiming the Word of Life. Let them empower inner city residents with the biblical training to defend their faith and teach sound doctrine.

Send out workers whose commitment to proclaim the Gospel exceeds that of evangelicalism. May their passion for the good news of Jesus Christ bring them to every inner city home. Let them save, equip and mobilize families to stay on the cutting edge of evangelism and to fulfill His Great Commission from their neighborhoods to the ends of the earth.

In Jesus' name, amen.

Divided Doctrine Inventory

1. Has past opposition or indifference by evangelicals to calls for social and political action limited your ministry's current vision for inner city outreach?

2. What factors determine the level of importance your ministry places on bringing sound doctrine to inner city men and women?

3. Action Steps: Brainstorm and list opportunities and constraints for the inner city harvest created by your ministry's doctrinal statement.

11 | Window of Shame?

Eighty percent of America's urban poor live in 105 metropolitan areas. Hampton Roads, Virginia, has the 28th largest urban population living in poverty in the U.S. I call this our 80/28 Window. Serving here exposes me to God's amazing power and His willingness to intervene on behalf of the impoverished families.

I have experienced our Lord's ability to thrust laborers (mainly myself) into the spiritual harvest, despite my efforts and others' to resist this assignment. As a result, I have seen God draw inner city families to Himself in places where white people seldom go and in circumstances that most cannot imagine.

Laboring in the inner city has blessed my life, because in the struggle I have experienced "all the energy of God working powerfully within me" (Col. 1:28). The Spirit of God opened this 80/28 Window for me.

Each time I witness God's incredible power to save, I am compelled to recruit more of His people into the spiritual harvest so that they might enjoy the wonders of His grace to save and of course bring people to Christ. Since God works in ways that put His glory on display, I have no doubt that anyone who walks by faith in Christ will experience His power.

God has gifted me as an evangelist. Along with this gift comes the responsibility to equip believers for this harvest. The opportunities are often overwhelming, so the need for laborers never ends. Surely other missionaries experience the same desire for equipping and mobilizing laborers. However, in my particular mission field there is a vast pool of Christian laborers who live nearby but do not realize how God might use them in this urban harvest.

Ironically, a misapplication of the **10/40 Window** missions strategy often makes mobilization of workers for the inner city more difficult. Policies that exist in missions organizations that de-emphasize ministry outside of the 10/40 Window contribute to the American racial divide and help perpetuate its devastating spiritual consequences at home and abroad.

If fulfilling Christ's purposes includes ministering in the inner city to neighbors who have suffered spiritually and physically from our neglect, leaving them out of our missions strategies magnifies the offense and adds to the many hurdles that the poor must overcome.

By defining our neighbors as those who live in a certain region of the world, missions leaders treat missions as zero sum game. This phrase means that they view Christian resources as finite so if they support missions in one part of the world then they must exclude other areas. This economic reasoning reminds me of the humanistic "values clarification" exercise from the 80's, which evangelicals denounced. Teachers would describe a lifeboat that could save six persons and then asked students to choose which six out of seven people of different backgrounds to rescue.

Taking the 10/40 Window strategy to this extreme makes decisions about missions funding easier but neglects justice and mercy for America's urban poor.

Glory or Shame?

As long as inner city communities remain neglected by missions strategies, I believe that this negligence brings shame to the name of Christ and tarnishes the Gospel. Bob Sjogren is a missionary author and President of UnveilingGLORY, a missions teaching and publishing ministry. He writes and preaches that God gets His greatest glory when He "unifies that which is diverse." The more divided the people groups are before Christ unites them, the greater the amount of glory received by God through the Gospel and the missionaries' efforts.

In a book co-authored with Gerald Robison titled *Cat and Dog Theology*, Sjogren describes this direct relationship between unifying racially diverse peoples and bringing glory to God.[1] As this unity/glory relationship is true and biblical, so the converse of this principle is true in that Christ's name is most dishonored when disobedience perpetuates racial division. The greater and longer that Christian neglect and segregation propagate the racial divide between blacks and whites, the greater the amount of shame this division brings to the name of Christ and His Gospel.

When evangelicals misuse the 10/40 Window to turn aside laborers from the inner city harvest, they turn their strategy into a window of shame that leaves many people of color around the globe still offended by American missions.

The 10/40 Window is an international missions plan emphasized by the AD 2000 Movement, which around 1990 started using computer-generated mapping to focus Christians on the most Gospel-needy places on the globe. The AD 2000 Movement used Matthew 24:14 and 10/40 Window maps to pursue the goals of evangelizing the world and seeing the return of Christ before the year 2000. This deadline has passed, giving evangelicals time to correct the unbalanced applications of this strategy that still undermine the mobilization of laborers for the inner city.

Territorial Grace?

Criteria for including countries in the 10/40 Window map have fluctuated a lot over the years. Subsequent mappings added certain countries and dropped others out of the Window with no explanation, while missions leaders debated what it meant to fulfill the Great Commission and how to include spiritually-needy areas that became canceled by neighboring Christianized locations. The number of nations included gradually doubled so the targeted band of nations no longer resembled a "window."[2]

Did God intend for churches to use the 10/40 Window strategy to focus the efforts of missions organizations and churches on a certain part of the world at the expense of our neglected inner cities? With such grave poverty of the masses in the 10/40 Window, can we justify spending one more dollar on ministry in the inner city, which we assume hears the Gospel in so many ways, when millions in other parts of the world have not even heard the name of Jesus Christ once?

My answer begins with the Lord of the Harvest. When He sends out laborers into His harvest, He makes all grace abound to the generous so that His sent ones have everything they need for every good work. Since He has not territorialized His grace - mission boards, denominations, churches, families and individuals must accept responsibility for ministering to inner city families *and* for sending laborers to the ends of the earth. We must trust our Lord for the capacity needed to accomplish both assignments.

The same goes for churches that exclude foreign missions by only funding outreaches to the needy around them. While ministering in the inner city, I must also keep the 10/40 Window on my radar screen, asking the Lord of the Harvest to send laborers, including workers of African descent, there.

Each missionary usually has a specific burden for a certain people group and rightly turns the hearts of sending Christians toward the spiritual harvest in specific places and cultures around the world. Nevertheless, my veteran missionary grandmother showed me how God's grace abounds for those in need both at home and abroad.[3]

C.S. Lewis warns that our spiritual enemies seek to direct the malice in the souls of Christians towards the people they meet every day, while wanting to send their benevolence to people on the remote circumference whom they do not know.[4] Therefore, we must be careful to defeat this scheme of the Evil One and show mercy at home and abroad, trusting in God's gracious provision to serve the entire world.

Consider this reasoning about inner city responsibilities and priorities. Past missionaries, sending boards and churches disregarded certain responsibilities for the sake of world evangelism that they are now reclaiming as priorities, trusting God's grace for the resources to fulfill them.

Many faith missionaries of the past, like my grandparents, received only enough money to get them on the field and meet their basic needs. As missionary kids, my aunt and uncle almost died from an illness in Africa because my grandparents had no resources raised to return to the States for medical care. My grandfather did not return to the States from Africa soon enough to receive medical care for repeated appendicitis attacks. His appendix burst as his ship approached Brooklyn and sadly he died at age fifty. Today, no modern missions agency or sending church would consider flying their missionaries around the world without significant medical contingency plans. Missionaries of previous eras also had to make more difficult parenting choices. For example, my grandmother in Africa chose to send my mom to a state-side boarding school during grandma's four-year assignments.

Fortunately, today's missionaries, boards and churches make missionary health, support and parental responsibilities higher priorities than in the past and plan for needed resources to cover them. Has the Lord's purpose to reach the lost changed or have we adjusted our priorities based on Scripture's commands to care for our families as well?

It is not an either-or proposition. We must evangelize the world *and* care for our missionary families. Similarly, we must also pursue God's purpose of showing mercy to our neighbors in the inner city. We must trust Him for the grace to fulfill our responsibilities to our inner cities, while we at the same time continue to send workers to the 10/40 Window.

In contrast, some churches' missions policies continue to neglect our inner city neighbors by using the 10/40 Window as a reason for not supporting local inner city evangelism. Certainly the Lord of the Harvest has the resources to fund all of His purposes. We now ask Him to fund health care and educational resources; can we not ask Him to fund mercy as well?

Re-evaluate the Issues

Presumably, the 10/40 Window strategically focused on difficult "missions fields" because too many missionaries had been targeting relatively easier, already reached people groups. The fact that inner city missions remains dangerous or difficult supports including them in strategies that mobilize workers for avoided fields.

Neglecting our inner cities while sending white missionaries overseas provides opportunities for Satan to defame Christ's Gospel by characterizing it as a white man's religion. Continued neglect of impoverished families because of our narrow focus on the 10/40 Window widens the racial divide. Just as the plight of the poor in northern ghettos motivated Dr. King to oppose the Vietnam War, in the same way evangelical neglect of the inner city poor can continue to alienate many African-Americans from Christ's mandate for world evangelization.

We must carefully analyze the thinking behind strategies that make reaching unreached people groups the sole criteria for funding decisions. How do we determine whether impoverished inner city families qualify as being "reached" or "unreached?" Are they "reached" because church buildings exist on most of their street corners and evangelistic preachers crowd the T.V. and radio broadcast spectrums?

Although the Gospel message virtually saturates American society as a whole, the uncorrupted Gospel often cannot penetrate the social and spiritual isolation of our inner cities. With Christ removed from public school holidays, with segregated churches promoting racialized doctrine, with liberalism in Black Theology and with the prevalence of generational family illiteracy, many inner city families have become disconnected and remain unaware of a clear and true message of salvation.

Spiritual opponents have further alienated inner city residents from Christianity by spreading false religions at growing rates in the last few decades.

Let me digress for a minute to illustrate a problem with labeling some inner city young people as "reached." I once took a group of ten teenagers to Philadelphia for a missions trip. We visited the Liberty Bell and the Betsy Ross Museum, where I began discussing Betsy Ross' role in history. One teenager began frowning and asked, "Did our country fight in a war against England? I thought England was our friend." I told him yes we fought two wars against England back in the 1700 and 1800's. He later asked, "Did we win?" This native son of historic Virginia did not know anything about the Revolutionary War!

For all the possible exposure to American history, this teen missed our nation's most celebrated victory. In a similar way, many inner city families remain unreached by the Gospel.

Since the Great Commission of Jesus Christ emphasizes making disciples (not just converts), an overwhelming number of inner city families also remain "unreached" by this standard. A year ago I attended an evangelistic Bible study in an apartment in the back of a public housing neighborhood with two young single mothers and their babies. A twenty-year-old young man in typical street gear pressed his face against the screen door and asked, "Ya'll studying the Word of God?"

At first, his description of the Bible as "the Word of God" indicated to me that he had been "reached." But after he walked into the living room to join us, I realized that I was wrong. He stopped for a split second before he sat down and unashamedly announced, "I don't read." He then respectfully participated in our discussion. He said he was looking for a way to get out of poverty since he had failed to graduate from high school and the Job Corps.

Is he "reached" because he knew about the Bible? Can I theologically justify asking for one more dollar towards evangelizing and discipling him? Would the considerable time it might take to teach him how to read the Word of God be worth the investment? Some may wonder why our Lord would ask us to spend time and money on this man when millions die around the world without ever hearing the name of Jesus.

Is not this decision up to the Lord of the Harvest? If He loves justice, then He will let grace abound for both. He reminds us in Luke 10 that the plentiful harvest belongs to Him.

Haiti's Example

A spiritual crisis in Haiti currently exists and provides another example of how statistically labeling a people group as "reached" fails to reflect their real need for the Gospel and laborers. In 1979, Kim and I prepared to go to Haiti to work in a network of missions outreaches that included churches, schools, a hospital and a radio station. The Lord changed our plans at the last minute but used our willingness to serve there to redirect us to Norfolk's inner city.

In the twenty-five years since then, Haiti's dangerous instability and violence forced many white missionaries who were stationed there to leave. Although missions statisticians describe Haiti as a "reached" country having a widespread dis-cipled Church,[5] the numbers indicate a greater level of need.

Eighty percent of Haitians are Roman Catholic and 55% of the population remains illiterate. Half are unemployed. Half practice voodoo, or in other words, are involved in the occult.[6] The life expectancy in Haiti is 49.5 years. Eighty-five percent of children do not complete high school. Despite the claim by some missions strategists that a widespread discipled Church exists in Haiti, illiteracy prevents evangelicals from equipping church leaders there.[7]

Where will missionary laborers come from to revive the desperate spiritual harvest in Haiti while most white missionaries cannot safely live and travel there? Mobilizing persons of African decent, who receive their missions survival training growing up in the inner city or third world environments, provides a practical solution.

I know uniquely prepared young Jamaican Christians seeking a window of opportunity to serve as missionaries in Haiti. But how can they preach unless they are sent?

Empower Persons of African Descent for World Missions

This mobilization to accomplish global missionary objectives creates appreciation for how well the Holy Spirit has prepared persons of African descent for missions. They have become culturally equipped for proclaiming the Gospel in many nations and have survived Satan's assault of political oppression, heretical teaching and immorality.

The Evil One has gone to great lengths to especially destroy inner city families' critical roles in fulfilling the Great Commission. Empowering persons of African descent for local and world evangelization tears down Satan's strongholds of racism and generates credibility for all messengers of the Gospel.

Dare we say that our Lord has failed to give His churches the resources to widen our missions window to include not only the 10/40 Window, but also our inner cities and the rest of the world? Jesus sees our bank statements and knows our capacity to support laborers for the harvest. Perhaps we fail to become "like springs whose waters never fail" for the poor overseas because we fail to show kindness to the poor in our own cities (Is. 58:11, Prov. 14:31).

Question about Responsibility

The issue of personal responsibility has been brought up a lot lately in the media, even among famous celebrities like Bill Cosby. How should Christians respond when questions arise about the behavior of the inner city poor? For example, if some people contribute to their state of poverty by behaving irresponsibly and destructively, does this misconduct end our mandate from Christ to sacrificially intervene?

In Jesus' parable of the Good Samaritan, the victim "fell into the hands of robbers" (Luke 10:30). Suppose he had abused alcohol, had "messed up" somebody's drug money or had lived in an immoral lifestyle and these behaviors somehow led to his becoming a victim to violence? Would the reason he became half dead change Christ's command to show him mercy? Would Jesus want us to drop him from our targeted window because he suffered from his own irresponsibility?

Before harshly answering these questions maybe Christians should watch *The Passion of the Christ* movie again. As depicted correctly in this movie, everyone's behavior during the Passion Week became more and more immoral and self-destructive throughout Jesus' arrest, trial, beatings and crucifixion. After grasping the magnitude of His suffering when Jesus died for our irresponsible sins, our gratitude should move us to share His great mercy with others who also need His forgiveness and saving grace.

Inner city families will not make positive transformations if we merely talk about their need to change their conduct. They will change when the Church meets them in their communities, intervenes in their lives with Jesus' transforming Gospel, disciples them to obey God's commands, and mobilizes them for the spiritual harvest through the Holy Spirit's anointing.

Missions Inventory

1. Evaluate whether your ministry uses the 10/40 Window strategy to justify neglecting the inner city harvest.

2. Evaluate your ministry's commitment to trust God for missions resources to reach families regardless of their location in the world.

3. How concerned is your church or missions organization about the mobilization of inner city families for world evangelization and the critical need for black missionaries in general.

4. Action Step: Make an appeal to leaders who oversee your ministry's missions committee to include the inner city harvest on their strategic planning agendas.

Step 3

Setting Critical Priorities for Joining the Spiritual Harvest

"Which now of these three, thinkest thou, was neighbor unto him that fell among the thieves?" And he said, "He that showed mercy on him." Then said Jesus unto him, "Go and do thou likewise." Luke 10:36-37

12 | Progressing through Passion

Yes, Father, for this was Your good pleasure.
Luke 10:21 (NIV)

This next strategic step of setting priorities for mobilization is like taking off from the first peak of a roller coaster. The previous two steps of expanding philosophy and analyzing the spiritual environment are similar to building inertia by steadily cranking the roller coaster's cars to the top of its highest hill.

This section launches the inner city venture by introducing the Lord's four critical priorities that thrust out laborers: passion, mercy, justice, and relationships. Once embraced, these priorities complete the needed evangelical thinking, in my opinion, about how and where to accomplish God's purposes and how to set His laborers on a vigorous course into an incredible spiritual harvest.

Two Aspects of Passion

Having passion increases the commitment, endurance and resiliency of inner city laborers. Actually, combining two aspects of passion, *heart and sacrifice*, gives the benefits I just mentioned. I call this combination "progressive passion," because one of these aspects builds on the other and together they yield better results.

Although some Christians are unnecessarily waiting for passion to grip them before becoming involved in the inner city, I believe that joining the inner city harvest depends more on how God uses progressive passion to mobilize His laborers. Before deciding where to minister, believers should understand how to combine these two different aspects of passion.

Rick Warren highlights the first aspect of passion in his book, *The Purpose-Driven® Life.* He asserts: "purpose always produces passion."[1] He goes on to teach that this aspect of passion refers to our heart-felt commitment for accomplishing a task that we love doing. It motivates us to excel with enthusiasm and effectiveness. Following the natural interests or inner promptings of our hearts helps us to find the type of ministry that God has designed us to perform.[2]

My great passion is teaching basketball skills and I love developing young players. Whether through AAU or high school junior varsity basketball programs, I find myself enthusiastically equipping young athletes to play the game because my heart is in it.

When ministering in the inner city, I discovered that passion for teaching basketball is also a valuable tool. It opens doors for me into the lives of inner city young people and therefore helps me lead them to Christ, address their educational problems, prevent immorality, stop drug dealer recruitment, evangelize their parents and establish churches.

Nevertheless, it has taken more than strong feelings for teaching basketball to sustain my ministry in urban Norfolk. When crack cocaine hit our streets in the 1980's and some of my former players began selling it, I could have easily pursued other options to coach in safer parts of the city.

I believe that God has given me the heartfelt desire to teach basketball skills for His glory, but I still had to choose where I would fulfill my passion for coaching. The spiritual warfare, persecution, criticism, exhaustion, disrespect and dangers associated with coaching inner city young people cannot be offset by passion for a sport. Some greater passion must sustain me and that is the passion to follow Christ. I must daily stoke the flames of this higher passion in my heart.

Changing the Status Quo

Left by itself, I believe that Warren's concept of heartfelt passion may actually limit involvement in the inner city. Deciding where to minister based on how passionately we feel about sacrificially serving the poor may lead to avoiding hardships and preserving structures that promote the status quo of racial separation. This is especially true for Americans from rural cultures who often value sameness and harmony.[3] Heartfelt passion must be combined with sacrificial conviction to mobilize laborers.

Status quo mentality in any culture increases the potential that believers will disregard Christ's command to love their neighbors because of its tendency to neglect the needy in favor of other priorities. For example, ghettos were established, and still exist, while white people - including white Christians - pursued their hearts' passions outside of the inner city and preserved the comfort and convenience of status quo racial and economic divides.

Sociological research reveals that white Christians still "ghettoize" spiritual leaders who confront racism. Rather than make sacrificial structural changes efforts to end racial segregation, this research shows that most white churches inadvertently isolate the voices that call for such changes.

Although giving these leaders mental assent or financial donations to address physical and spiritual needs of the urban poor, most white Christians do not want to be inconvenienced by the cultural upheaval that would be associated with tearing down the racial divides in their churches. This ghettoizing phenomenon prevents the confronters of racism from impacting these racialized structures and, in effect, silences them, even though they try to speak up.[4]

If we "follow our hearts" without understanding how traditional structures restrict the focus on where and with whom we carry out our passionate ministries, we may unintentionally perpetuate this status quo racial divide.

Christian leader Francis Schaeffer warned against remaining part of the Silent Majority made up of persons motivated by two bankrupt values: personal peace and affluence. By personal peace he means, "just to be left alone, not to be troubled by the troubles of other people, whether across the world or across the city."[5] Christians who silently pursue these two heart-felt values above justice and mercy continue to enable the existence of evangelical structures that ghettoize the poor.

Tom Skinner described the results:

And make no bones about it: the difficulty in coming to grips with the evangelical message of Jesus Christ in the black community is the fact that most evangelicals in this country who say that Christ is the answer also go back to their suburban communities and vote for law-and-order candidates who will keep the system the way it is.

So, if you are black and you live in the

black community, you soon begin to learn that what they mean by law and order is, "all the order for us and all the law for them." You soon learn that the police in the black community are nothing more than the occupational force present in the black community for the purpose of maintaining the interests of white society.[6]

Although without the malice of past generations, white Christians may also justify their lack of personal involvement in the inner city based on this passion concept. They may excuse neglect of justice and mercy by concluding that that they do not have the same passion as those "called" to inner city ministry or as those who confront racial division.

James H. Cone in *Risks of Faith* (1999) condemns the silence of white theologians and challenges them to learn about and speak against "racism and its brutal impact on the lives of African people." Appalled at their silence, Cone asks, "Where are the white theologians?"[7] His question, in my opinion, challenges white evangelicals to take a stand for righteousness.

Perhaps white theologians speaking from the inner city have not been heard because they get ghettoized along with people who fall outside the mainstream passions of Christianity. One reason this might occur is because many evangelical churches that I have observed do not appear to sense responsibility for evangelizing the inner city neighborhoods near them.

Jesus Christ has asked us to implement a harvest in an ocean of need. His command requires personal risks and sacrificial service. Death for this cause is not out of the question.

A white theologian recently proposed a resolution that members of a certain denomination send their children to private, Christian schools. This may shield their children from the ills of society, but what about those left behind? Who will passionately apply Christ's command to love them?

On the other hand, what would happen if denominations voted to provide Christian school education to inner city children at the same level of sacrifice that they make for their own children? How else could they love the children of the inner cities as themselves?

Sacrificial Passion

I believe that it is critical for Christians in the Body of Christ to begin allocating their talents and resources according to the core values given by the Lord of the Harvest. To follow Him, believers must attach importance to giving unconditional love, service and self-sacrifice regardless of how passionate we feel about a cause.

Although Warren's concept of passion helps each of us define our ministry according to our unique makeup and desires, obeying Christ's commandment to love also requires that we sacrificially extend mercy to our impoverished neighbors. To do so I believe that we must discover and embrace another aspect of passion demonstrated by Christ.

The word "passion" itself comes from a Latin word for suffering and Christ's passion refers to His suffering and death.[8] Jesus learned through pain and suffering how to obey His Father and how to perfect justice.[9] Therefore, His passion describes the magnitude of His commitment to glorify His Heavenly Father through suffering.

Mel Gibson's movie, "The Passion of the Christ," shows the brutality endured by God's Son as He responds to His Father's plan in perfect obedience. From its beginning scenes that depicted Jesus in the Garden of Gethsemane, Gibson illustrated passion as Christ sacrificially "humbled Himself and became obedient unto death, even death on a cross" (Phil. 2:8).

When combined, these two aspects - heart and sacrifice - form a progressive passion that mobilizes workers for the inner city harvest far more effectively than either could alone. The passion of Christ promotes mercy and justice by motivating us to contradict our natural inclinations for survival.

It builds upon the concept used by Warren because it takes our heart-felt ministry passions and focuses them on spiritually-motivated obedience that defies our emotions. It compels us to love Christ more than life itself and fills us with compassion that transcends the natural inclinations of our hearts.

This progressive passion motivated myself and some believers I know in Norfolk to provide cutting-edge educational therapy to inner city children at a cost they would not be able to afford otherwise. In partnership with the **National Institute for Learning Disabilities (NILD)**, we established the **Park Place School**, which works with inner city children who are challenged with learning problems.

Because the school has a high cost/student ratio, convincing Christian donors that this school is worthy of their financial support remains one of our most formidable obstacles. Yet many Christian families make severe personal sacrifices to provide educational solutions for their own children.

In obedience to Christ's command that we love our neighbors as ourselves, we should find it reasonable to sacrificially provide solutions for the educational problems of inner city children in the same ways we help our own.

Christ's command to love inner city children like we love our own seems like a set-up for failure because it costs so much to carry it out. Only Christ can provide the passion necessary for sacrificial evangelism in the inner city harvest.

Therefore, we must recognize and stir up in us the two aspects of passion that work together to mobilize workers for inner city outreach. The "passion of the Christ" must motivate His people to use their unique ministry passions to serve sacrificially where they have no natural inclination to go or normal feelings of concern for the residents. As disciples of Jesus Christ, we must also gratefully obey His command to love our inner city neighbors by pursuing God's priorities of justice and mercy.

Scripture exhorts us to: "Fix your eyes on Jesus . . . who for the joy set before Him, endured the cross, despising its shame, and sat down at the right hand of the throne of God" (Heb. 12:2). Jesus delighted in passionate sacrifice to obey His Father. This passion for obedience compelled Christ to endure horrible suffering and die on a cross.

By faith and through His grace we must likewise joyfully and sacrificially follow Him in love to break down the divides that keep evangelical Christians out of the ghettos. We must humble ourselves "even unto death" because of our passion *for* the Christ.

We must mobilize in spite of fleshly passions that the status quo offers in racially segregated Christianity. Jesus promised to remain with us as we obey His commission. His divine presence and power assures us that inner city evangelism is not only possible, but will be accomplished through our obedience.

Since in the past many white evangelicals used doctrines of God's sovereignty and providence to justify slavery by assuming that its existence suggested divine approval, conservative Christians should recognize their tendency to use rationalizations to protect status quo social order.[10]   Evangelicals today must challenge unbiblical reasoning that excuses continued neglect of their responsibilities to personally evangelize and empower inner city families.

Passion Inventory

1. Does your passion in life bring you closer to, or farther away from, the inner city harvest?

2. How do the location and focus of your passion impact status quo racial divides?

3. In what ways does Christ's passion of self-sacrifice mobilize you for ministry?

4. Action Step: Brainstorm ways to relocate and live out your passion so that pursuing it brings inner city families to Christ..

13 | Evaluating Your Thinking

Rarely do we find men who willingly engage in hard, solid thinking. There is an almost universal quest for easy answers and half-baked solutions. Nothing pains some people more than having to think. Martin Luther King, Jr.[1]

"Mercy-driven purpose" describes an additional priority that God uses to successfully mobilize laborers for the inner city. Before understanding this factor, believers who step up to the plate must face some painful thinking about trendy evangelical ideas. For example, they should consider what Martin Luther King Jr. might think today if he could find only five purposes in the book, *The Purpose-Driven® Life*.

Would he conclude that Warren falls short of including the priorities of mercy and justice when explaining the purposes of God? Have evangelicals thought solidly enough about these purposes to make sure their answers are not too easy and that their solutions are not half-baked?

Contrasting Warren and Cone's conclusions about white Christianity encourages us to contemplate the incompleteness in typical evangelical thinking.

In a previous book that he wrote, Warren labels five purposes of God, which he describes in *The Purpose-Driven® Life*, as membership, maturity, ministry, missions, and magnify. Consider "membership" with its purpose - "You were formed for God's family"[2] - and compare Cone's experiences with white church membership.

Cone writes in *Risks of Faith*:

> What puzzled me most during my childhood about the religion of Jesus were . . . the conspicuous presence of the color bar in white churches. In Bearden, like the rest of America, Sunday was the most segregated day of the week. Black and white Christians have virtually no social or religious dealings with each other, even though both were Baptists and Methodists – reading the same Bible, worshiping the same God, and reciting the same confessions of faith in their congregations. Although whites posted 'Welcome' signs outside their churches, ostensibly beckoning all visitors to join them in worship, blacks knew that the invitation did not include them.[3]

> The Church . . . is a ministry to middle-class America! How else can one explain its snail-like pace toward an inclusive membership? Even though Paul says that Christ "has broken down the dividing walls of hostility" (Eph. 2:14); the Church's community life reflects racism through and through. It is still possible to be a racist, a black hater and at the same time a member of the Church.[4]

Fellow evangelicals may dismiss Cone's indictment because of his liberal doctrine. We might reject his doctrinal prescriptions for healing our ailing body of Christ because he has rejected the authority of Scripture. But though we reject a suspicious remedy, we should carefully consider the truth in this doctor's diagnosis.

No matter how menacing Cone's doctrinal threat might seem to us, we must not carry on doing nothing about the inner city poor as if the body of Christ is healthy and then succumb to pharisaical spiritual blindness in our ignorance. Painfully thinking about racism's impact on the way we apply our list of God's purposes, we must ask, "Did Warren half-bake the purpose-driven® life?"

King said, "If everyone is thinking alike then somebody isn't thinking."[5] At the risk of being dismissed with Cone, let me at least give him credit for helping me raise the question: "Are we thinking?"

Unfortunately, Cone argues for liberation thinking as the alternative to the evangelical five purposes of God. While Warren anchors these purposes to our eternal destiny, Cone shows how these purposes lost credibility because Christians used them to oppress:

The black intellectual community is becoming increasingly suspicious of Christianity because the oppressor has used it as a means of directing the oppressed away from any concern for present inequalities by emphasizing a heavenly reality beyond time and space. Naturally, as the slave begins to question his existence as a slave, he also questions the religion of the enslaver.[6]

A Difficult Diagnosis

Evangelicals must think hard and long about Cone's statement. We must accept the truth that some white Christians who have sought to excel in Warren's five purposes have also oppressed others by practicing racial discrimination. Whether oppression comes through malicious actions or from silence, the results are devastating and the consequences eternal.

Though we cannot accept Cone's conclusions about bringing justice by denying evangelical doctrinal essentials, we dare not miss the hard reality of his analysis. His diagnosis helps us recognize the inadequacy of how we have defined the purposes of Christ and challenges us to complete our conceptions of Christ's teachings.

If evangelicals define five purposes of God, then we must accomplish them through mercy or we become guilty of injustices. Unfortunately, Cone dismisses the fundamental doctrines of the Bible along with the sinful behavior of those who disregard and violate them.

If as evangelicals we hold to doctrines that we deem necessary for spiritual life and eternal salvation, and if our practices or neglect have resulted in the slave and the poor rejecting these doctrines, then we bear responsibility for corrupting the Gospel of Jesus Christ. If persons seeking liberation from our racialized structures turn to another gospel, then our racism and our silence during racial division destroys the faith of many.

I believe that the consequences for our neglect have been far more brutal than liberal theologians have claimed. In their doctrinal framework they can only condemn us for making hell on earth. But if we hold that those who reject the essentials of our evangelical faith - even those who stumble over white evangelical racism - spend eternity in hell, then our faith in the

Biblical essentials condemns us more severely. According to our own doctrine, this neglect makes us guilty of ushering our impoverished neighbors towards the Lake of Fire.

Warren hurts my ability to explain the repentance of white evangelicals and the progress we have made in racial justice. He testifies in *The Purpose-Driven Church* that his congregation fulfills its mission by targeting white middle class males who fit a profile he calls "Saddleback Sam."[7] The replication of this marketing strategy by white or black churches that target one race of people over another must provide black intellectuals with enough evidence of racial discrimination to continue discounting and ignoring evangelical doctrine.

Using this homogeneous church growth strategy in more diverse communities demonstrates that churches still condone structural segregation because they target one race over another. Apparently not much has changed since Cone's childhood observations of the "color bar" in the white church. What are we thinking?

For decades, homogeneous church growth strategies have made comfort and growth in numbers their first priorities and have enabled churches to justify keeping the color bar. These strategies usually generate church structures that attract persons who feel comfortable in racialized atmospheres.

Fortunately, younger Christians, who generally interact more with persons of other races in today's diverse society, now feel comfortable in multi-racial churches. Research indicates that multiracial churches have begun growing faster than homogeneous churches. I believe that multi-racial congregations will soon become the churches of the future as their younger believers minister within their racially and culturally diverse networks of relationships.[8]

Many white evangelicals need a good dose of mercy-driven reality. Without emphasizing mercy and justice, the well-scripted five purposes of God continue to fuel the fires of those who deny Jesus Christ by supporting their argument that evangelicals neglect these priorities. I have seen the eternal consequences in the inner city and in Jamaica. As a critical success factor for mobilizing workers, applying the concept of "mercy-driven purposes" requires believers to reason through the issues facing inner city evangelism.

The spiritual harvest among most of our country's unchurched urban poor occurs on family porches, in living rooms, at kitchen tables, outside back doors, in community centers, on streets and at schools. When ministering with unchurched inner city families, I know in advance that I will need to spend much time with them in their neighborhoods before they will attempt to respond to my invitations to attend seeker services.

This process challenges assumptions that the harvest should occur only in church buildings. As Ralph Neighbour, who founded Touch Outreach's cell group movement, points out in his book, *Where Do We Go From Here?*, constructing facilities to attract families is a rural church growth strategy that fails in our world's expanding urban cultures.[9]

Thinking Inventory

1. How much thinking has your church done about including mercy and justice as priorities for accomplishing God's purposes?

2. What precautions has your church taken to avoid neglecting the inner city harvest when emphasizing fulfilling Warren's five purposes of God?

3. Action Step: Meet with another ministry leader to talk through the need to make mercy and justice foundational priorities for accomplishing God's purposes.

14 | Learning From an Expert

We need an expert on God's purposes to help us examine the concern about making mercy a priority, and Luke 10:25 provides one: "On one occasion an expert in the law stood up to test Jesus. 'Teacher', he asked, 'What must I do to inherit eternal life?'" Although we may criticize this expert for testing Jesus, we may benefit from applying Christ's response.

A few Bible commentators view the expert's test question as an acceptable way for a student to address a teacher in Christ's day. Perhaps this expert stood up because he was thinking and wanted to know God's truth. We might even put ourselves in his shoes and rephrase the question for Jesus as, "What must I do to completely fulfill your purposes for my life?"

For those of you unfamiliar with Luke 10, Jesus responds to the expert's question with a question, "What is written in the Law?" Fortunately, the expert knows the Word of God and answers, "Love the Lord your God with all your soul and with all your strength and with all your mind;" and "Love your neighbor as yourself" (10:26). Jesus compliments the expert of the law on his answer by saying, "You have answered correctly."

The expert's answer might have impressed evangelicals today. He quoted the Old Testament proof texts that Rick Warren uses to define the purposes of God in his books, *The Purpose Driven Church* and *The Purpose Driven® Life.* Warren, like Jesus, called these passages the greatest commandment. They not only summarize the Old Testament Law but also encompass four of the five purposes of God for our lives today (magnify, membership, maturity and ministry).

Warren's remaining fifth purpose, "You were made for a Mission"[1] comes from Christ's **Great Commission** in Matthew 28:18-20, which most evangelicals consider to be the ultimate way to love one's neighbor.

Status Quo Thinking

Wanting to make sure that he had fulfilled the Law of God completely, the expert goes on to ask Jesus in verse 29, "Who is my neighbor?" This question addresses the thinking of that day that loving one's neighbor referred only to those persons who were like them and who lived near them.

When living in Jerusalem, the Jews there thought that the Law required them to just love the neighboring Jerusalem Jew. When living in Galilee, they thought that the Law required loving the neighboring Galilean Jew, etc. With this narrow definition used by the Pharisees, their interpretation of the Law required no love for the Gentile, and especially no love for enemies like the Samaritans and Romans.

The thinking of the day did not include these hated groups in the definition of "neighbor." Status quo thinking absolved religious Jews of responsibility for the plight of anyone outside their restricted definition of the word "neighbor."

Our expert helps us think when he asks Jesus' theology on this word "neighbor." In seeking to justify himself, perhaps the expert sought to make sure that he had completely obeyed the Law of God. In any event, Jesus' parable of "the Good Samaritan" in Luke 10 made the expert rethink his traditional understanding of God's purposes. This story not only cuts across the thinking in the expert's day, but it should challenge believers today to think painfully hard and differently from the current evangelical status quo. Do we leave out a critical command when compiling our list of God's purposes because we miss the point of this parable?

Fulfilling God's Purposes in the Bloody Way

Jesus goes on to describe in Luke 10:30 the plight of a beaten man on the road between Jerusalem and Jericho. The expert hearing this story would immediately relate to the danger on this journey. At the time, about 1,200 priest or Levites lived in Jericho and made the trip back and forth between Jerusalem to fulfill their annual assignments at the temple.

Called "the Bloody Way" because of the violent attacks by robbers who waylaid its travelers, the road from the mountains of Jerusalem to the Jordan plain provided ample opportunities for ambush. Resembling the mountain passes on cowboy television shows where bad guys wait to attack unsuspecting wagon trains, the terrain of the Bloody Way made the journey notoriously dangerous.

Fulfilling the Law of God put many priests and Levites on this road. Beyond the intense education required to acquire expertise and teach the Law of God in Jericho, they traveled twice a year to serve for a week in Jerusalem. They also risked the journey at other times for Jewish festivals.

Priests and Levites had opportunities to obey the greatest commandment and lead the nation of Israel in fulfilling the same five purposes described in *The Purpose-Driven® Life*. As they secured their own homes before making the difficult journey to Jerusalem, they may have, as the Law required, ministered to the needs of their neighbors. As they packed up and endured their journey through the dangerous Bloody Way, they may have prepared their hearts to love the Lord by singing or chanting psalms. They may have prepared their bodies for temple service by avoiding any unclean person or thing that would disqualify them.

When in Jerusalem, the priests and Levites may have expressed love to the Lord through purification, burning incense, worship, prayer and reading the Torah. As they ministered to God's people, cleaned the Lord's house, made sacrifices and interfaced with Gentile worshippers and pagan representatives of the despised Roman Empire, they may have served as God's witnesses to the lost world. All of their ministries could have tied into Warren's forty days of purpose. By following the five purposes of *The Purpose-Driven® Life's* and using the status quo definition of "neighbor," the expert may have felt justified.

In Jesus' story, however, the sight of the badly beaten man who Scripture says was half dead on the roadside did not even apparently slow down the priest or the Levite! They both simply stepped aside and continued on their journeys.

If the expert hearing this story imagined these two religious leaders on their way to Jerusalem, he might have thought of many reasons why they were justified for their neglect. Stopping to help the victim would have jeopardized their lives because the thieves might still have been hiding nearby. Finding him dead would have made them ceremonially unclean, which according to God's Law disqualifies priests and Levites from performing their services in the temple without first making expensive and time consuming sacrifices.

Finding the victim alive would require them to take time to assist him. Since the Temple operated on an elaborate schedule of rituals and shifts, any delay might have kept them from performing important spiritual duties. During a festival season, Jerusalem would be too crowded for them to find a suitable place to take him anyway.

If the expert imagined the priest and Levite in Jesus' story on the way home from service in the temple, he might have rationalized that they were caught off guard by the needy one. The expert knew that these two officials, having served faithfully in the temple to complete the five purposes of God, would have been focused on getting safely through the Bloody Way.

He might have excused their neglect of the man on the road by concluding that they were preoccupied with the thoughts of well-earned rest, a reunion with loved ones and ministry with their "real" neighbors back home in Jericho.

In either case, the expert probably envisions two spiritual leaders finding a beaten-down man outside of their temple's facilities, outside of their programmed services, outside of their mission statements and maybe outside of their race and culture.

He knew that stopping and helping would require the priest and the Levite to risk their lives, to impose upon their families, to interfere with ministry duties, to possibly have to spend two days wages, to risk overspending their budgets, and worst of all, to blow their schedules!

Jesus' story allows the expert to see how conventional thinking hijacks the purposes of God. Clearly, the beaten man did not meet the status quo definition of neighbor held by the religious leaders of that day. As a result, the priest and the Levite passed by without thinking about their responsibilities to intervene. Jesus shows the expert how "half-baked" conventional purpose-driven® thinking had become!

After describing how the Samaritan stopped to rescue

the beaten man, Jesus asks the expert in verse 36, "Which of these three do you think was a neighbor to the man who fell into the hands of the robbers?" Jesus' question challenges the expert's status quo thinking.

Because Jews despised Samaritans, some commentators think that the expert of the law could not bring himself to answer, "the Samaritan," so he replied, "The one who had mercy on him."

By making a hero out of someone who does not conform to the temple's theology, program, network, and status quo way of thinking, Jesus emphasizes the forgotten biblical priority: "God saves you to show mercy!" Jesus asked the expert to think about His question and then He commissions him to a life of fulfilling God's mercy-driven purposes by saying, "Go and do likewise" (11:37 NIV).

Cone and others charge white evangelicals with failing to extend mercy in this manner in America's inner cities. Evangelicals have stepped aside to walk right past similar needs and continue to step aside with devastating consequences. If we do not elevate mercy to its rightful place in the purpose-driven® life, how will we receive mercy from the Lord? Would not Jesus value mercy before magnify, membership, maturity, ministry and mission?

The Great Commission

Some evangelicals might attempt to include extending mercy under their purposes of ministry or mission. Then why not make membership a subpoint under maturity? Why not make mission a subpoint under ministry? Why not make ministry a subpoint under magnify? We describe each of the five purposes separately because they carry so much weight in our thinking. Does not mercy carry as much weight?

Would not extending mercy trump any of these five purposes of God? Can we ignore the suffering of our inner city neighbors and remain members in good standing with our churches? Can we step aside and reach spiritual maturity? Can we step aside and minister in the power of the Holy Spirit? Can we step aside like the priest and the Levite in Jesus' parable while we send missionaries around the globe? Can we magnify the Lord of the Harvest while disregarding our neighbors who live in the inner city?

Does not the Lord of Micah 6:8 exalt mercy before the five purposes in *The Purpose-Driven® Life*? Does not the Lord of the harvest command us along with the expert in the law: "Go and do likewise"?

Evangelicals cry out against liberal theologians, politicians and judges. We flee public school systems. We despise abortionists. We rebuke Jehovah Witnesses. We oppose Islam and especially the Nation of Islam.   None of these share our faith in God's Word and the Lord Jesus Christ. Yet Jesus' parable condemns us instead of them.

Although these unbelievers do not share in our churches, our programs or our salvation, they all stop and show mercy to our poor while we step aside and walk past them. Like the expert who avoided saying that the "Samaritan" had accomplished God's purposes, Jesus makes us swallow the same difficult pill regarding those whom we condemn but who have made mercy for our poor their mission through the years.

I believe that Jesus would say to us today from our beloved Word of God, "Go and do likewise!" A commission from Jesus for evangelicals to follow the examples of compassionate humanists would be a most ironic turn of events, since

Schaeffer and other Christian leaders have condemned them for destroying our country's Judeo-Christian values.

For the sake of hard thinking, let us expand Jesus' parable to include many generations of African-Americans in the "Bloody Way." Imagine that they had been stripped and beaten down by robbers for four hundred years. Factor in what would happen if the robbers used the religion of the priests and the Levite to teach submission through these years.

What would the victims think about the priests and Levites as they watched them pass by in silence for four centuries? What would they think about this religion that refused to consider them as neighbors and love them with actions and not mere words? What would you expect them to think about the Bible when those who robbed them used it to justify their oppressive ways? Whose religion do you think this race of victims would believe, the priest's or the Samaritan's? Is it any wonder that most African-American leaders support liberal theology and liberal politics?

Segregation practices of evangelicals and insensitive policies of conservative politicians during our country's history drove African-Americans away from the authority and values of God's Word.

Tom Skinner made this point at Urbana 70:

Understand that for those of us who live in the black community, it was not the evangelical who came and taught us our worth and dignity as black men. It was not the Bible-believing fundamentalist who stood up and told us that black was beautiful. It was not the evangelical who preached to us that we should stand on our two

**feet and be men, be proud that black was beauti-
ful and that God could work his life out through
our redeemed blackness. Rather, it took Malcolm
X, Stokely Carmichael, Rap Brown and the
Brothers to declare to us our dignity. God will not
be without a witness.**[2]

Jesus leaves it to His listeners to imagine the spiritual consequences for the priest and the Levite who ignored and passed
by the beaten down man. I believe that God wants us to assess
the spiritual and eternal consequences of past and present
racism and neglect.

Will not believers be held responsible for all those of
African descent who turned away from the precious Gospel of
Jesus Christ because evangelicals offered it corrupted and distorted by racism, oppression and silent neglect? Will not
Christians give an account for all the peoples in the world who
consider Christianity an oppressor's religion, as demonstrated
by evangelicals' treatment of blacks? Will policy makers and the
silent associates of Bible colleges and seminaries suffer loss for
preventing African-Americans from attending their schools and
for all who missed hearing the true Gospel preached because of
this segregation? Can congregations today be filled with the
Holy Spirit while ignoring the plight of their neighbors?

Might not Jesus confront evangelicals today as He did
the Church in Pergamum, "You remain true to my name; you
did not renounce your faith in Me . . . Nevertheless, I have a few
things against you . . ." (Rev. 2:13,14). Because of continued
neglect of the inner city harvest, the Judgment Seat of Christ
may turn out differently than evangelicals expect, especially if
Jesus applies this parable to the neglect of our nation's poor.

Neighbor Inventory

1. Do inner city families fit in your definition of neighbor?

2. How have you fulfilled your responsibility for showing mercy to your neighbors in the inner city?

3. Action Steps: Write down the names of five persons who need Christ but who are not open to the Gospel. Pray for their salvation and for opportunities to serve them as a committed friend.

15 | Making Mercy Your Priority

Thus saith the LORD, "Let not a wise man glory in his wisdom, neither let the mighty man glory in his might, let not the rich man glory in his riches: but let him that glorieth glory in this, that he understandeth and knoweth Me, that I am the LORD which exercises loving-kindness, judgment, and righteousness in the earth: for in these things I delight," saith the LORD. Jeremiah. 9:24

Seeking to fulfill our mission with clear consciences before God, how should evangelicals respond to Christ's command in Luke 10 to show mercy? What actually did He mean by mercy? In our attempts to show mercy, how do we also promote justice?

Biblical understanding for mercy-driven ministry comes from Jesus' teachings and example, the theology of God's goodness and other commands and promises in Scripture.

Jesus' Teachings about Mercy

In addition to addressing the expert's questions, the topic of mercy came up in many of Jesus' interactions with the

Pharisees.   Although valuing the Law of God, they had left mercy off of their list of God's priorities.

Jesus confronted their failure by demonstrating real acts of mercy that often violated their own rules and regulations. On one occasion, Jesus ate dinner at Matthew's home with tax col- lectors and other kinds of "sinners."   (The Pharisees looked down on tax collectors as cheats and traitors.) The Pharisees, obviously feeling spiritually superior, criticized Jesus for associ- ating with such people.

Jesus responds by quoting from Hosea 6:6 and giving this command: "Go and learn what this means: 'I desire mercy, not sacrifice'" (Matt. 9:12 NIV).

This challenge to the Pharisees has significant implica- tions for understanding the commission to show mercy in Luke 10, where Jesus discusses the parable of the Good Samaritan.

By quoting Hosea 6:6 in Matthew 9:12, Jesus elevates the meaning of mercy. He uses the Greek word *eleos* to trans- late Hosea's Old Testament Hebrew word, *checed.* His inter- change of these words supports the interpretation that he also meant *chesed* when He referred to mercy in the Good Samaritan passage.

Chesed means more than taking pity or showing kind- ness to those in need. It is the wonderful, enduring covenant love that the LORD bestowed on His people throughout the Old Testament. Christ connects this Greek word for mercy, *eleos,* with the rich meaning embodied in the definition of *checed* given by Ryrie in the notes of his study Bible: "It means loyal, steadfast, or faithful love and stresses the idea of a belong- ing together of those involved in a love relationship."[1]

The biblical context of the Good Samaritan parable is "love your neighbor as yourself" and supports taking mercy to this higher definition when Jesus commands: "Go and do like-wise." Jesus clearly commissions His disciples to establish rela-tionships with desperate people based upon merciful love.

When declaring, in Matthew 9:12, the Lord's desire for "mercy, not sacrifice," Jesus definitely meant showing *chesed* mercy to sinners. For He added, "It is not those who are healthy who need a physician, but those who are sick." Christ makes mercy-driven evangelism an over-riding priority for pleasing and glorifying God. Later in Matthew 23, Jesus not only exposes unmerciful pharisaical thinking on a personal level, but He also reveals how it infected their theology and religious programs.

He makes this clear while sharply condemning the Pharisees in Matthew 23:23: "Woe to you scribes and Pharisees, hypocrites! For ye pay tithe of mint and anis and cummin, and have omitted weightier matters of the law, judg-ment, and mercy and faith: these ought ye to have done, and not to leave the other undone."

The Theology of God's Goodness

The bond of belonging together in a relationship of love characterizes *checed* mercy and distinguishes it from benevo-lence. For example, God's benevolence does not oblige Him to enter into ongoing love relationships with those in need "for He causes the sun to rise on the evil and the good, and sends rain on the righteous and unrighteous" (Matt. 5:45).

Entering into covenant relationships with sinful people through this kind of mercy cost God most dearly because it required the atoning death of His Son. In contrast, God's benev-olence comes from His infinite storehouse of resources. When one considers how God's self-sustaining, infinite power is avail-able to Him for showing goodness to His creatures, it becomes apparent that He gives benevolence at relatively little cost to Himself. Checed mercy, on the other hand, requires of Him this loyal, steadfast relationship of love where God becomes personally bonded with destitute persons to redeem them for eternity. This *chesed* relationship cost Him the sacrificial death of His beloved Son on a cross.

With this distinction made between mercy and benevolence, believers should evaluate whether their outreaches fulfill Christ's mercy-driven mandate or not. Although they greatly benefit many in times of emergencies, soup kitchens, food drives and homeless shelters that supply provisions and sermons with no bond of relationship are mostly acts of benevolence and not mercy ministries.

They may make the Christians feel merciful, but without the love relationship with those in need these kinds of ministries do not fulfill Christ's command to show mercy. Whereas benevolence is often funded from the wealth of those who give and is administered in ways that are most convenient to them, mercy's bond of love requires personal and sacrificial intervention on the part of those who truely connect with the needy.

Jesus told the Pharisees to learn how to unconditionally accept their sinning neighbors enough to bond with them in a steadfast relationship of love. He knew that this kind of mercy outreach had to be caught by experience and not just taught as a principle. He exemplified relationship-based evangelism for the Pharisees and for His disciples.

Christ intentionally cut across the traditions of men and theological thinking of His day by establishing relationships with sinners. For example, He met Matthew at his tax collector's booth, unconditionally accepted him, bonded with him in his home, and then evangelized other "sinners" through Matthew's network of relationships. Christ willfully broke pharisaical teaching on more than one occasion to exalt the value of mercy. Healing a man's withered hand on the Sabbath is another example (Matt. 12:1-14).

Old Testament Commands and Promises about Mercy and Justice

Explaining the significance of God's mercy in Scripture would require countless books! Hundreds of verses proclaim that God's *chesed* endures, empowers and remains forever welded to truth, justice, and worship. For example, David wrote that we may sing of the mercies of the LORD forever. Through these passages, Old Testament scripture overwhelmingly proclaims relationship-based mercy as the fundamental priority upon which we accomplish the purposes of God for our lives.

The Old Testament also clearly makes justice an essential for fulfilling God's purposes.[2]

Besides mercy, God commands His people to include justice in their mission statements. Consider Micah 6:8: "He has showed you O man, what is good. And what does the LORD require of you? To act justly and to love mercy and to walk humbly with your God."

This verse summarizes the LORD's requirement that His people *asah mishpat,* meaning to *accomplish, make and produce* justice. *Mishpat* emphasizes the judicial protection of rights. The KJV often translates this word as "judgment," while the NASB usually translates mishpat as "justice."

Another common Hebrew word for justice, *tsadaq,* refers to being and doing right. It is often translated as righteousness. Both words find similar usages in the Old Testament. Hebrew poetry sometimes pairs them. They merge into the

New Testament Greek word, *dikaios,* translated righteousness or justness. The related forms of these words: just, justly, justification, justifier, right and righteous have these same meanings.

Mercy and justice are the central themes of the true Gospel message.[3] God purposed from the beginning that His people would become ambassadors of this reconciliation. Because God first loved us, in gratitude we should make justice happen through mercy's loyal, committed love. In other words we should engage in committed relationships with others less fortunate than ourselves and protect their rights.

Scripture records how God required His people of faith to act justly and to love mercy while His plan of salvation unfolds in the Bible. Since our Lord acted justly when saving us and again by commissioning us to show mercy, we must weigh our priorities and values against His Word.

George Yancey, an evangelical author and sociologist associated with the Willow Creek Community Church near Chicago, provides a Christian definition of racial reconciliation that he calls "reconciliation theology." An important principle of his ideology calls for Christians of all racial and political backgrounds to challenge social structures that promote racial inequality and division.[4]

The Appendix consists of a list of actions for correcting systemic injustices that are still imbedded in many evangelical social structures.

Mercy-Driven Inventory

1. Evaluate whether your outreaches are driven by true "chesed" mercy that bonds believers with urban families in relationships that create a sense of belongingness.

2. Questions to ask yourself:
__ Do I have Jesus' passion for mercy and justice?
__ Do I value these priorities as the conditions for genuine church membership, maturity, ministry, mission and even worship?
__ When I show mercy, do I offer loyal, steadfast, or faithful love that stresses belonging together in a love relationship?
__ Do I really love mercy or do I participate in projects that just make me feel merciful?
__ Do I confront systemic injustices?
__ Do I have a conscience sensitized by Christ's command to show mercy?

3. Identify benevolent outreaches in your ministry that help members feel merciful but fail to sacrificially establish long-term relationships of mercy with the poor.

4. Action Steps:
Prayerfully review the action steps listed in the Appendix for ending systemic injustices. Check those directly associated with your ministry and ask God to use you as a change agent. Meet with leaders to appeal for action.

Budget three hours a week in your schedule for friendship time with unbelievers. Ask someone to join you in this discipline and hold each other accountable to keeping this investment of time a priority in your schedules.

16 | Devoting Your Resources

> . . . what is better–will not be taken away from
> her. Luke 10:42 (NIV)

Our Lord gives each of His laborers only a certain amount of time and energy to dedicate to His harvest. For this reason, Jesus counsels Martha in Luke 10 on how to strategically devote these entrusted resources to developing mercy-driven relationships as priorities that yield lasting results:

> Now it came to pass as they went, that He entered into a certain village: and a certain woman named Martha received Him into her house. And she had a sister called Mary, which also sat at Jesus' feet, and heard His word. But Martha was cumbered about much serving, and came to Him, and said, "Lord, dost Thou not care that my sister has left me to serve alone? Bid her therefore that she help me." And Jesus answered and said unto her, "Martha, Martha, thou art careful and troubled about many things: But one thing is needed: and Mary hath chosen that good part, which shall not be taken away from her (Luke 10:38-42).

Jesus enters Martha and Mary's home where they express their devotion to Him in different ways. Martha takes the initiative to show mercy to Jesus by preparing a full-course meal for her traveling friend, worrying over the details.

Luke 10:40 explains how Martha becomes distracted by too many preparations for their dinner, while Mary listens at His feet. The Greek word describing Martha's distraction indicates that her mind had become overly occupied with taking care of so many concerns at the same time that she does not know which to attend to first.[1] Overwhelmed, she is drawn away from the most important part of hospitality, which is her relationship with her guest.

Although Martha's work temporarily meets the need of food for all present, she shows feelings of resentment towards Mary and complains to Christ. Jesus responds to Martha's frustration by stating that only "one thing" is necessary. Bible commentators disagree on the meaning of this statement and usually support one of the two following interpretations:

1. Choice of Needs. Some limit Jesus' meaning of the words "one thing" to the sisters' choices between physical and spiritual food. They conclude that mankind's only real need is learning the Word of God or spending time with the Him. Some support this interpretation by assigning to the phrase "one thing" a higher meaning in an attempt to give the words more spiritual significance.

Applied to the inner city harvest, this view sheds some light on the conflicting ministry extremes that white Christians have tried with African-Americans since the Civil War. While evangelicals preached the Gospel, they emphasized spiritual needs but neglectfully ignored oppression and poverty. Liberals addressed poverty by focusing more on physical rather than spiritual needs. Like Martha, both found fault in the other camp's unbalanced viewpoint.

2. *Choice of Devotion.* Earlier commentators conclude that Jesus' admonition referred to Martha's preoccupation with making too elaborate a meal, which robbed her of valuable time with Him. He counseled her that a one-course meal (only one thing) would have sufficed, freeing her to focus like Mary on Him or His teachings.

Jesus apparently uses a "play on words" about food when He says that Mary chose the "good part," alluding to the portion of honor that an important guest is given at a banquet. Jesus did not say that she chose the only part, but the most honorable component of their devotion to Him. He indicates that Martha should have invested less time and effort on preparing food for their meal and chosen to show her devotion by allotting more time to listening to Him.

Although she settled for less than the best way of showing devotion to Christ, the following commentaries find some value in appreciating Martha's ministry:

> **Our Lord's rebuke is not aimed at hospitality, not at a life of energy and business. It is intended to reprove the fussy fretfulness which attempts many unneeded things, and ends in worry and fault-finding. It does not set a life of religious contemplation above a life of true religious activity, for contemplation is here contrasted with activity put forth with a faulty spirit.[2]**

Both were true-hearted disciples, but the one was absorbed in the higher, the other in the lower of two ways of honoring their common Lord. Yet neither despised, or would willingly neglect, the other's occupation. The one represents the *contemplative,* the other the *active* style of the Christian character. A Church full of Marys would perhaps be as great an evil as a Church full of Marthas. Both are needed, each to be the complement of the other.[3]

These conclusions, which appreciate both action and contemplation, are supported by Jesus' instructions in Luke 10 to show mercy to neighbors and by other commands in Scripture regarding hospitality.

To apply this interpretation to ministry with the poor, consider how impoverished persons often get treated as the Church endeavors to show them mercy. Since Jesus taught that persons who assist the "least of these" in reality express their love to Him, let the needy replace Jesus in this story to evaluate how Christians give mercy today.

Good Efforts. Trying to show mercy, many Christians invest time, money and energy in activities and programs that do not create opportunities for establishing personal relationships. They might provide good services, but without long-term follow-up and family outreach many of these programs bring only temporary benevolence.

Soup kitchens, food and clothing closets, one-night homeless shelters, special events, Thanksgiving baskets, Christmas present giving, thrift stores and clinics may miss this most important ingredient of evangelism. Inner city families often see programs come and go with the Christians who produce them.

Better Relationships. Jesus commended Mary for choosing a more enduring way of showing devotion. He valued the time that she spent listening to Him. Mary's choice is similar to valuing relationships over activities in evangelistic mercy. Examples of outreaches that develop friendships to bring lasting changes include: home visitation, personal evangelism, new-believer follow-up, one-to-one discipleship, neighborhood canvassing, evangelistic Bible studies and church small (cell) groups.

Best Combinations. By telling Martha in verse 37 that only one thing is necessary, Jesus admonishes her for being overly busy. This same principle applies to ministry among the urban poor. Jesus encouraged Martha to design her ministry activities to *strategically* meet needs in ways that make relationships a priority. He emphasizes the importance of designing activities that create room for establishing relationships, not detracting from them.

Combining programs that address physical needs with relationship-based outreaches increases the impact of both. Examples of programs that effectively support relationship development include those related to: Graduate Equivalency Exam (GED) preparation, adult literacy, after school tutorial and mentorship, summer camps, sports ministries, youth clubs, drug/alcohol recovery meetings and housing outreaches.

Making relationship-based evangelism the objectives of these programs increases the likelihood that they will succeed. To begin effective ministry among the urban poor, consider the following evangelism principles that parallel Jesus' counsel to Martha as she attempted to serve Him:

Principle: Relationships of trust provide the best means for evangelism and give long-term, effective results. How often do most Christians sit at the feet of impoverished families to listen to them and to learn how to effectively minister? I have observed over the years that many Christians feel uncomfortable with witnessing anywhere because they fear saying the wrong things and getting rejected.

Fortunately, Jesus commands us to show mercy through relationships and not cold-turkey debates. He usually began His personal evangelism by asking questions. Jesus demonstrated how listening and relationships take evangelism to a higher level of effectiveness.

The advantages of witnessing like Jesus did through relationships become more obvious when reaching inner city men with the Gospel. Since women and children primarily respond to outreach programs, evangelizing men usually requires additional strategies. Often the best strategy involves going into the homes of the women served by programs to make a concerted effort to meet and build trust with the men in their lives.

Husbands, ex-husbands, boyfriends, brothers, male cousins, fathers, step-fathers, and other male friends of the family are there to be found and reached by developing relationships with them beyond the program-based efforts.

Access to men is critical for success but outreach ministries often neglect them by limiting the focus of their programs to serving mothers and children like these men do not even exist. Making men a priority becomes possible by working through relatively extensive networks of inner city relationships.

Touch Outreach Ministries, founded by Ralph Neighbour, is an example of one ministry that promotes evangelism strategies that emphasize relationship networks. The large networks of friends, neighbors, co-workers and relatives in the inner city should be identified, joined and expanded to spread the Gospel.

Since most people come to Christ through relationships, Satan will try to convince us that befriending unbelievers is a waste of time. He will tempt us to invest our time in other activities, especially those that seem more spiritual.

By investing in relationships, we receive the blessing of becoming "spiritually pregnant" with persons as the Lord gradually draws them to Himself through our friendships. The Lord allows us to carry friends to full-term, anxiously praying for them like an expectant mother awaiting the birth of her child.

The Lord blesses the witness of those who follow up on the spiritually newborn and fulfill Christ's commission to make disciples. Relationship evangelism increases the likelihood that Christians will care for new believers. Discipleship becomes a natural extension of the friendships that begin prior to the new believers' commitment to Christ. The bonds of discipleship between new believers and evangelists often become cemented during conversion as their relationships bear fruit. Since Christ commissioned us to teach obedience to His commands, the evangelists' relationships with new believers provide opportunities for spiritual accountability, guidance and protection.

Relationships also promote justice. As Christians become involved in the lives of persons in need of mercy, they begin to experience life from their perspective. The more disciple-makers walk in the shoes of those in need, the more they begin to notice the systemic injustices that often frustrate the impoverished. When empowered persons ask questions about these roadblocks, they may begin seeking ways to bring about justice. Many questions came to my mind as I began pursuing relationships with the urban poor.

Relationships provide awareness of systemic barriers and motivate Christians to change institutionalized structures that prevent mercy and frustrate justice. Dr. Beverly Daniel Tatum says that this new and probably uncomfortable awareness by whites often comes by having close relationships with blacks who suffer injustices. It is an important step that whites can take towards abandoning racism.[4]

Learning from the poor, just like Mary learned by listening to Jesus, shows them respect, gives them true mercy and brings about the lasting results valued by Him.

Principle: Time and location constraints must be carefully evaluated to improve relationship development by strategically optimizing these resources, since some distractions are unavoidable. Luke 10:40 described Martha as a person distracted by all the preparations necessary to provide a nice meal. She apparently made these preparations in another room while Mary sat at Jesus' feet. Consider how the typical good strategy for church outreach in the inner city reduces the availability of laborers for relationship evangelism because of time, place and personnel constraints:

1. Build (or rent) buildings.
2. Develop specialized and comprehensive programs to get families into these buildings.
3. Recruit volunteers or hire people to run programs.
4. Hire administrative professionals to supervise them.

5. Market the programs.
6. Repeat building project once or twice until the church or ministry runs out of land or money.
7. Offer additional specialized programs for the poor.
8. Recruit more people to run these programs.
9. Hire more administrative professionals to train and supervise volunteers.
10. Market the programs.

These strategies, although popular and useful, provide good results but may distract churches from making a higher-level, longer-lasting relational impact in the inner city harvest. Building projects provide vision and excitement as members take financial steps of faith and roll up their sleeves.

Commitment to building-centered evangelism usually will not last much longer than the time as it takes to complete the new facility. Subsequent building maintenance rarely incites evangelistic zeal. The building also immediately defines a church's methodology and potential for inner city evangelism by setting in cement, as it were, its program capacity and location.

Although a building becomes a necessary distraction to community evangelism, the level of distraction depends on church leaders' and members' determination for keeping evangelism relationship-oriented and neighborhood-centered. Expanding a building gives new opportunities for evangelism but still does not promote, by itself, the best means of outreach.

Buildings provide a valid way to serve Christ and a place for seekers to find Christ. But when buildings consume too much time for members and keep them away from places that promote relationship development with unbelievers, buildings unavoidably distract from the most effective evangelism.

When programs, likewise, consume believers' time that might be invested in relationships, then churches have settled for good, but less than the best, evangelistic impact. Persons in church music programs with multiple choirs, special music, instrumentals, pageants, plays and bells, for example, often have little time and energy to invest in relationships with unbelievers and neglect the most effective means of evangelism.

The problem is compounded by the additional time constraints of Sunday Schools, other missions outreaches, youth ministries, nurseries, sports, camps, breakfasts and small groups, plus evangelism programs like concerts, Evangelism Explosion activities, bazaars, rallies and children's clubs. When we factor in the extensive time demands of Christian schools and the committee meeting assignments from all of these programs, it is obvious that time and place limitations deter many from acting justly and showing mercy, particularly with unbelievers.

In my opinion, time constraints caused by too many "activities" and programs have demobilized churches from effective relationship evangelism for some time. According to Francis Schaeffer, many evangelical leaders did not become involved in his public stand against abortion, infanticide and euthanasia because they did not want to disturb other projects.[5]

I have also observed how time and program constraints have prevented most evangelical leaders from becoming personally involved in mercy-driven evangelism. If churches make the success of programs their primary objective, they may inadvertently choose to implement good outreaches instead of the best kinds. Programs require high levels of administrative skill and energy to attract participants. Evangelists without strong administrative gifts often burn out trying to mobilize their churches for outreach by implementing complicated programs.

Churches may try to solve this dilemma by assigning administrators to run the programs, even though they may not have the gift of evangelism needed to equip God's people.

Marketing church programs to unbelievers makes far less impact on the outside world than strategies that build relationships with them outside of the church walls. Word of mouth and face-to-face contacting, the most difficult types of marketing, create the best results because they are based upon or lead into relationships of trust.

If buildings and programs dominate the evangelism vision of churches, how do they reach their cities except by starting new building projects and new programs? Norfolk has approximately 200,000 residents and about half are white and half are black. How big must existing churches become to evangelize the entire city?

Obviously, these churches' building capacities become constraints. To reach an entire city under the program/building vision, the construction and programming must be repeated. Since the demands of this repetition consume time and other resources necessary for relational evangelism, the best form of outreach may get neglected in this kind of vision. These churches may become increasingly isolated from unbelievers while trying to build Christ's kingdom.

Positioned properly, programs and buildings may positively impact evangelism by generating support and maintaining real relationships. They meet felt needs, which open the door to relationships, but must be followed by concentrated relationship development to have lasting impact.

Most programs are not designed to promote the personal follow-up of new contacts and converts because this kind of relational investment is harder to administrate and requires long-term commitment. Some programs follow up new believers and guests through mailings. Although better than no follow-up at all, these impersonal attempts to appear friendly cannot compare with making real relational connections with new believers.

Shepherds of the flock must look seriously at how members invest limited ministry time. They must weigh the tradeoffs of recruiting people for programs versus mobilizing them for community evangelism. Church leaders must evaluate their own time investments in relational evangelism if they want their flocks to make this a priority in their lives.

The Evil One constantly works to distract believers from the harvest. If he can get churches to invest their time in maintaining building-based programs, he prevents them from investing in the best means of reaching the lost.

Although many Christians seek churches with the most comprehensive family programs, these programs cannot substitute for relationship development in evangelism. To reach their evangelism potential, churches must mobilize believers for relationship development, not program maintenance.

Unfortunately, mobilizing members for relationship development is much harder than recruiting them for programs. Mass appeals such as sign-up lists or pulpit and bulletin announcements effectively convey information about the programs and work well for recruiting volunteers. Program recruits may be trained in seminars and Sunday School classes.

In contrast, relational outreach skills must be caught rather than learned in classroom settings. Persons are equipped while observing and interacting with evangelists who are engaged in relationships with unbelievers as their lifestyles. Relational discipleship breeds relational evangelists who invest their lives in serving unbelievers and in equipping new believers to do the same.

Without conscious efforts by leaders to preserve this multiplication process, program saturated church environments will short-circuit this chain reaction of relational evangelism and discipleship. A balanced evangelism strategy makes relationship development a priority while strategically designed programs and buildings support the development of these relationships.

Philip: the Biblical Role Model?

If the Lord of the Harvest values relationship evangelism combined with mercy and justice, then these three dynamics should characterize the life of a scriptural evangelist. One would expect a role model for evangelism to act justly, love mercy, serve the needy, cross divides created by racial prejudice and value relationships.

Although Ephesians 4:11 indicates that many gifted evangelists edified local churches during the first century, we find only one, Philip, specifically named in the New Testament. In Acts 21:8-9, Luke identifies Philip as "the Evangelist" and as "one of the seven" when recording how the Apostle Paul stays at Philip's house in Caesarea during his last journey to Jerusalem.

This description, "one of the seven," refers to Acts 6:1-7 where Philip qualifies as one of seven servant-leaders in the new church in Jerusalem who are "known to be full of the Spirit and wisdom." What mighty feat defined this man of God's first ministry? Did this Spirit-filled evangelist preach a crusade and lead thousands in the sinner's prayer?

No, Philip's first distinguishing ministry was serving neglected widows by waiting on their tables so they might receive mercy and justice. This evangelist, with six other men, fed the needy and healed relationships in the church, freeing the apostles for "prayer and the ministry of the Word." Philip fulfilled Martha's work so that Mary's priority could abound.

After persecution scatters the Jerusalem church, Acts 8:4-8 reports how this evangelist is the first to cross the racial divide of his day. Instead of black/white animosity, persons of Philip's time and race bitterly hated and segregated themselves from a people called the Samaritans, whom they considered inferior.

Philip obeys Jesus' command to witness across this divide, becomes anointed with power as He proclaims the Christ, defeats the forces of darkness and heals the "paralytics and cripples." He brings mercy, justice and joy to an entire Samaritan city.

Acts 8:26-40 highlights Philip's relationship evangelism skills. Obedient to an angel of the Lord, Philip heads south from Jerusalem on the road to Gaza. While on route the Spirit speaks to Philip and sends him to stand next to an Ethiopian official who is sitting in his chariot reading the Book of Isaiah.

At the Ethiopian's invitation, Philip climbs into the chariot, sits down and successfully conducts the first recorded evangelistic Bible study. Like Jesus, Philip begins his anointed witness by asking a question. He then rides the spiritual wave that the Holy Spirit creates for him and leads the Ethiopian to Christ.

Finally, the Scripture records how Philip's lifestyle contains qualities essential for successful relational evangelism. After the Holy Spirit takes Philip away from the Ethiopian, the evangelist "traveled about, preaching the gospel in all the towns until he reached Caesarea" (Acts 8:40). Since he fearlessly travels and conducts fruitful "cold turkey" evangelism, why does Philip settle at Caesarea?

Perhaps the Holy Spirit purposefully makes Philip a role model for relationship-based evangelism. In addition to earning the reputation as an evangelist, Acts 21:8-9 says that Philip acquires a house in an important, racially-diverse seaport, raises four spiritually gifted daughters and shows hospitality to the Apostle Paul and his traveling companions. This information suggests that this evangelist valued and invested in long-term, mercy-driven relationships.

"Eight Ball:" A Modern Testimony

This year, I received a welcomed call from Chris Williams, someone who had been converted to Christ through my camp outreach, who is serving in full-time ministry at a residential drug treatment center in Alabama.

During his childhood, his mother and the man living with her heavily abused drugs. His mother turned to Christ after this man died from an overdose. As often is the case with the youngest child of a drug abuser, Chris coped by behaving like a clown and acting wildly. He did not participate in sports like his older brothers.

He appeared disinterested in the Gospel until he came to our summer camp when he was 14 and took my small group Bible study seriously. He made a commitment to Christ one night as we sat in the dark behind the camp lodge on number-ten cans that I had borrowed from the kitchen.

In the years following this decision, his inner city neighborhood erupted into a proliferating drug market and Chris dropped out of school to sell crack. His intense involvement earned him the notorious nickname "Eight-ball," which is street slang for two grams of cocaine.

When his drug dealing and abuse spun Chris's life out of control, two retired white middle-class couples used their relationships with his family to intervene. Curt and Trudy Kenney and Bob and Peggy Diehl had developed friendships with Chris and his mother through our camping and tutorial ministries, which also linked his extended family to a local church. Curt and Bob pursued Chris for many months, seeking opportunities to help him end his self-destructive behavior.

The turning point came when police raided the neighborhood one night. Chris had drugs and a gun in his possession when he saw an officer running towards him with arms extended. Instead of subduing Chris, this officer ran right past him! Chris was the only young man among his peers who did not get arrested that night.

He went home and made a vow to change, if God would make a way. A week later Curt and Bob arrived at his apartment. After an initial failed attempt, they managed to take him to a residential drug treatment ministry two hours away from his home. God worked mightily in Chris's heart and eventually gave him a Christian wife, children and a fruitful ministry.

Chris calls me now and then to express gratitude for how we made a difference in his life. God answered our many prayers for Chris by using both program-based outreaches *and* committed relationships to intervene in his life.

Relationship Inventory

1. Which of these two principles seem the most difficult to implement?

___ Relationships of trust provide the best means for evangelism and give long-term, effective results

___ Time and location constraints must be carefully evaluated to improve relationship development by strategically optimizing these resources, since some distractions are unavoidable

2. What programs in your ministry need to be combined with relationship evangelism?

3. What relationship evangelism may be better fueled by outreach programs?

4. Actions Step: Draw a flow chart to show how your ministry's programs and relational evangelism complement each other.

17 | Transforming Your Structure

White church leaders seeking to attract inner city neighbors to their meetings often focus on providing culturally "inclusive" worship, meaning they use music and worship styles that appeal to different ethnic or racial groups. Presuming that African-Americans, and persons of other races, stay away because of different tastes in music, they rely on syncopated beats to make Christ, His Word, and His Church more culturally attractive to the community.

Some churches/ministries radically change their music to follow King David's example when he brought the ark of the Lord to Jerusalem and "danced with all his might," while praising God using the 96th Psalm ("Sing to the Lord a new song").

A closer look at this psalm provides the motivation to go farther than just changing worship approaches to attract different types of people. Here the Holy Spirit glorifies Jesus Christ by celebrating an occasion greater than David's festivities. David sees beyond his days on earth, past the times of the Bible's prophets, past the first coming of Jesus, farther than our own current era of history and forward to the second coming of our King: "Then all the trees of the forest will sing for joy; they will sing before the LORD, for He comes, He comes to judge the earth. He will judge the world in righteousness and the peoples in His truth" (Ps. 96:12,13 NIV).

From this vantage point, Psalm 96 commissions God's people to a lifestyle of evangelism until our Lord arrives: ". . . praise His name; proclaim His salvation day after day. Declare His glory among the nations, His marvelous deeds among the peoples . . . Say among the nations, 'The LORD reigns'" (Ps. 97:2,3 and 10 NIV).

This commission includes making these wonderful invitations to the families of the nations: "Ascribe to the LORD, O families of the nations, ascribe to the LORD the glory and strength. Ascribe to the LORD the glory due to His name; bring an offering and come into His courts. Worship the LORD in the spender of His holiness; tremble before him, in all the earth" (Ps. 96:7-9 NIV).

Changing musical rhythms or cultural slants to connect with inner city families is just the beginning when attempting to reach then with the Gospel. In obedience to this psalm's directives, churches wanting to minister cross-racially to inner city neighbors should "turn the beat around" in structures other than just musical methodology. The following seven strategies turn church structural beats around to line up with the heartbeat of Jesus Christ as depicted in Psalm 96:

1. *Expand members' prayer lives to include inner city neighbors.*
   A. In obedience to Jesus' command in Luke 10:2, mobilize members to specifically ask the Lord to thrust out laborers for His harvest in the inner city.
   B. Encourage them to pray through Psalm 96 and boldly entreat the Lord to keep the church family on the cutting edge of His spiritual harvest there.

C. Lead the church in intercession to tear down strongholds of injustice, immorality and neglect, which exist inside and outside of its doors.

D. Have members stop and pray whenever the media reports on inner city issues.

E. Emphasize the need to pray that God saves and sends out men from the inner city.

F. Engage the congregation in spiritual battle against the forces of evil.

G. Identify neighborhoods by name when calling on members to pray.

H. Find ways to creatively encourage members to pray consistently and intelligently for the inner city harvest.

I. Ask members to include requests for the inner city on their personal, daily prayer lists.

J. Financially support urban missionaries who solicit prayer for the lost there.

K. Publish names of public housing and other low-income neighborhoods and encourage members to visit them to learn how to pray specifically.

L. Include prayers for the churches, government agencies and businesses in these communities.

2. *Revamp strategic planning to include urban families.* Strategic planning that makes mercy-driven outreach a core value composes a new structural song in the spirit of Psalm 96, rather than the same old song of offering programs that only give temporarily results. To accomplish this aim, leaders must first embrace this core value and reflect it in their mission and vision statements.

The following planning exercise builds upon the inventories at the end of earlier chapters. Leaders fill in the following table with statements that summarize strategic plans before and after making ministry to inner city families a core value. This endeavor also gives churches opportunities to strategically elevate the role of evangelists whom the Lord would use to edify laborers as He thrusts them into His harvest. Leaders may evaluate, redesign or scrap programs that do not focus on building relationships to create new outreaches that facilitate friendships with unbelievers.

Added Core Value: Mercy-Driven Ministry with the Poor										
	Personal		Family		Church		Business		School	
	Before	After	Before	After	Before	After	Before	After	Before	After
Mission										
Vision										
Objectives										
Goals										
Accountability										
Challenges										
Action Steps										

Although broadening the mission and vision statements of local churches and Christian schools to value serving inner city families may seem like formidable structural leaps of faith, envision leaders of these ministries someday giving an account to the Lord for not including impoverished neighbors in their strategic plans and schedules.

3. *Rearrange schedules to proclaim the Lord's salvation day after day.* To make relationship evangelism possible, congregations must streamline personal and church schedules to free up time for cultivating friendships. This adjustment begins with the Lord's Day to take advantage of opportunities that exist because unbelievers spend time together on Sundays, especially in inner cities.

As the son of a minister, I grew up faithfully attending four meetings every Sunday, not including weekly choir practices and youth groups meetings. In the years prior to 1990 I was maintaining this same kind of meeting schedule until I refocused my efforts on church planting. So when we began the Urban Community Church, I anticipated experiencing a spiritual decline in my relationship with the Lord when I simplified my Sunday schedule to devote more time for establishing new relationships in the inner city.

When I first readjusted my activities, my church planting ministry consisted of leading a Sunday morning cell group meeting, teaching a Monday evening Bible class, and maintaining discipleship relationships. I also picked up a foster teenager on Sunday afternoons and we hung out with families in the inner city, sharing the Gospel when the Lord gave us opportunities.

Instead of feeling spiritually deprived by my new schedule, I became revived when I prearranged time for evangelism. I grew closer to Christ and to other believers. Our new church eventually scheduled one celebration service on Sundays and encouraged members to use their free Lord's Day time for relationship outreach. Ironically, during this evangelism I was able to keep up with more NFL games than usual as I spent Sunday afternoons relating to inner city men.

Lacking musical ability, coupled with our desire to avoid

being labeled by a certain worship style, we waited for the Lord to send in persons with the talent and worship skills to properly lead multi-cultural, inclusive celebration services. Our small group of believers entered into intense worship and praise without music for one year. We simply read back the Psalms and other scriptures to the Lord as an offering. Our worship occasionally became emotional as some expressed their gratefulness to God through tears of joy.

In addition, we equipped new believers to obey Psalm 96 by demonstrating how to worship the Lord before unsaved friends and neighbors through personal evangelism. Eventually, the Lord provided skilled praise team members who led corporate worship while faithfully maintaining high commitments to proclaim His salvation.

I adjusted my personal schedule by increasing my time involved in relational evangelism and decreasing my time in scheduled church service. This change helped me apply Jesus' counsel to Martha in Luke 10 and establish relationships with unbelievers just like Christians use these verses to encourage spending time with the Lord.

Churches may also apply this passage to evangelism and release their members from program obligations, which may be good ministries in and of themselves, to give them more free time for outreach.

Although opening Sunday schedules for relationship evangelism tests the values of congregations and their leaders, this change also provides these leaders more time to set good examples for their members.

Evangelists should implement discipleship processes in the church body life that encourage members to include spending time with unbelieving neighbors in their weekday schedules.

Dr. George Yancey, a sociologist who consults with churches on multiracial dynamics, recommends creating multi-racial congregations having inclusive worship by expanding members' racially diverse social networks through friendship evangelism.[1] This kind of outreach requires accountability among Christians who expend their time and energy in other pursuits and places than evangelism and the inner city.

Most of us stay so busy that we must keep disciplined schedules to free us from distractions and to protect our time for developing relationships with non-Christians. Task oriented individuals must strategically schedule time for these relationships.

I made the same kind of commitment for our four children as they progressed through elementary school. When they were too young for school, I scheduled a morning each week to take them out for a special activity. I protected this time by crossing it out on my calendar, considering myself unavailable for any other scheduled appointments.

In the same way, believers need this kind of goal-oriented focus to protect time in their schedules for evangelistic relationships. Christians must prayerfully organize their schedules and seek accountability to join the Lord's inner city harvest. Turning the beat around to sing the new song of Psalm 96 requires scheduling relationship times as non-negotiable priorities. Time management is a strategic component of effective relational evangelism.

4. *Equip members with relational evangelism skills that transfer to inner city outreach.* Since these skills are caught rather than taught, church leaders should implement discipleship-based training to equip and mentor members in relational evangelism. Once mastered, the members may use them to

connect with inner city families. This discipleship-based training takes each person through the following four equipping stages:

Stage 1: Follow-up. Leaders show and teach members how to share their faith as they follow up new contacts from church services, outreach events, programs and para-church ministries. This discipleship training becomes an early step for equipping new believers. Churches maintain databases to monitor new contact follow-up.

Stage 2: Friendship Evangelism. Leaders use Touch Outreach Ministries' strategies (materials available at its web site) to equip members to reach persons in their circles of influence. Members then learn how to increase the number of unsaved friends in these circles by establishing new relationship networks with them.

Stage 3: Cell Group Evangelism. Leaders also use Touch Ministries' strategies to equip small groups to facilitate relationship evangelism.

Stage 4: Multiplication. Members equip others through these four stages of discipleship-based relational evangelism.

Church members prepared in this way will be ready for the best kinds of cross-cultural relationship-based evangelism.

5. *Invest in church body life that praises the LORD before unbelievers, declaring among them that He reigns.* As Ralph Neighbour teaches, Christians should invite unbelievers to exchange their worldly lifestyles for new relationships with

Christ and His family. Strong relationships between church members make this exchange attractive.

"Cell" churches have an advantage because their demonstrations of love for Christ and other believers in home gatherings witnesses for Christ. In the context of these relationships, members may invite unbelievers to spend time with the Lord and His family, not to just attend a building or programs. In this way, they represent Christ as His ambassadors and avoid becoming church salespersons.

Whereas churches usually make their Sunday Schools the focal point of body life, in our experiences, offering formal Sunday morning classes at church buildings has failed to evangelize the inner city poor. Many impoverished families live accustomed to staying up Saturday nights and sleeping in on Sundays. They usually do not own dress-up clothes and lack transportation, including the several car seats required for their small children. Single mothers may need to get as many as five children ready for church without help. Some inner city adults have less than fond memories of sitting in classrooms.

In contrast, community-based group meetings on Sundays or during weekday evenings have overcome these problems and have created relationship bridges between inner city families and churches. Neighborhood weekday Bible studies have given unemployed single mothers opportunities to hear the Gospel without distractions from their children who attend school or camps during the day.

6. *Judge programs based on their support of relationships*. Leaders must apply standards based on true mercy when evaluating the effectiveness of an outreach program. As we saw in Luke 10:39-40, churches may miss the best kinds of evangel-

ism by serving somewhere other than the homes of inner city families. Most churches serve the poor through outreach programs in their own facilities like soup kitchens, food drives, homeless shelters, substance abuse meetings, clothes closets, tutoring, youth outreaches and sports teams. Christian non-profit organizations add more extensive programs like affordable housing, health clinics, thrift stores and GED programs.

7. *Empower Inner City Leaders.* As I said before, churches with the vision to appreciate leadership potential in the inner city men will reap eventual growth. When God matures these men and anoints their ministries, they become valuable role models who attract families from like backgrounds and races. Churches wanting to attract inner city neighbors must invest in men from there, providing training and ministry opportunities even while these men are new believers.

Community evangelism and outreach programs provide excellent opportunities to empower, equip and mobilize inner city leaders. Inner city residents have proven effective in opening doors for evangelism through their existing networks of relationships in their neighborhoods.

They also have made successful canvassers and leaders for establishing neighborhood evangelistic Bible studies and cell groups. Empowering inner city families by employing them in outreach programs gives them opportunities to grow in Christ and to fulfill His Great Commission at home and abroad.

Since inner city programs require skilled workers who recruit and serve residents, churches and non-profits should hire and train residents from these communities to serve in their own neighborhoods. In doing so, they provide an effective means for developing more relationships for church outreach. Many inner city converts must work two jobs at low wages to provide for their families as Christ intended. By hiring them to run their programs, churches unleash them for service, discipleship, biblical training, evangelism and missions.

Investing in ministry jobs for home-grown leaders capitalizes on their community relationships for the sake of evangelism and makes discipleship multiplication a priority. Programs also free up time for these leaders to follow up on new believers and connect them with local churches.

Structural Inventory

1. What strategies from this chapter have been implemented in your ministry?

___ Expand the prayer lives of church members to include inner city neighbors.

___ Revamp strategic planning to include inner city families.

___ Rearrange schedules to proclaim the salvation of the LORD day after day.

___ Equip members with relational evangelism skills that transfer to inner city outreach.

___ Invest in church body life that praises the LORD before unbelievers, declaring among them that He reigns.

___ Judge programs based on justice and truth.

___ Empower leaders from the inner city.

2. Action Step: Fill in the table provided in Strategy 2 of this chapter to describe your personal, church and school's mission statements before and after making the inner city harvest a core value.

Step 4

Creating Momentum by Implementing a Plan of the Lord

And into whatsover house ye enter, first say, "Peace be to this house." And if the son of peace be there, your peace shall rest upon it . . . Luke 10:5-6

18 | Beginning Your Outreach

Jesus' Luke 10 evangelistic project provides a practical evangelism tool to begin making lasting relationships that cross race and class divides. Borrowing from Frank Tillapaugh's wisdom in his book *The Church Unleashed*, up to this point I have emphasized philosophy and strategy rather than methodology to give principles that are transferable to each ministry's unique situation. Tillapaugh supports presenting methodology when it primes the pump and provides innovative and workable ideas.[1]

After centuries of neglectful silence in segregated structures, evangelicals seeking to mobilize for the inner city harvest will greatly benefit from discovering innovative pump priming methodologies like this one described in Luke 10. In addition, Dr. Beverly Tatum warns that raising white people's consciousness of racism without providing them tools for moving forward may place them at risk of feeling stuck in their anger.[2]

This section offers the Luke 10 project as an effective method for moving forward while joining the inner city harvest.

In the March 15, 2004 issue of *U.S. News and World Report* the American trend of increasing participation in Bible studies was reported on. In its article, "Hooked on the Book," reporter Diane Cole explains how people want to know what is in the Bible, especially those having relationships with conservative Christians.[3] An interest in learning about the Bible is currently an excellent open door for evangelism in the inner city.

In my opinion, home evangelistic Bible studies are the best way to begin relationship-based inner city outreach. Churches and outreach ministries may follow Christ's strategy in Luke 10. By canvassing targeted neighborhoods and asking their residents, family by family, if they would like to study the Bible in their homes, churches may begin new outreaches. Then by working through the "man of peace" (described later in this section) the churches may reach entire neighborhoods through these Bible studies.[4] These studies can then merge into a neighborhood cell groups that can either develop into a new church or just tie in with the body life of an existing church.

At Urban Discovery Ministries, we used an evangelistic Bible study to establish an inner city cell church at the same time Ralph Neighbour began publishing materials about his Touch Outreach Ministries cell church model in the early 1990's. His writings affirmed the lessons we had learned in the inner city. We decided to follow his strategies and use his training materials. They proved very helpful in equipping inner city residents for relationship-based evangelism. Since then, several more authors have joined Ralph Neighbour in offering extensive equipping materials, which I recommend.

To support our church plant we also established community programs in these neighborhoods to meet felt needs. These programs increased our circle of relationships for expanding relational evangelism. We designed a **Graduate Equivalency Diploma** (GED) outreach, summer youth camps, recreation teams and mentoring programs to quickly build relationships of trust with members of entire families.

The recreation teams involved children and attracted men. Visiting as coaches rather than "ministers," we usually received a positive reception when making home visits.

Ministries may also partner with **Project Light Inc.** to provide a learning center model that uses relationship-based, one-to-one GED and literacy tutoring to reach inner city adults.[5] The relational evangelism supported by these programs should continue as the first priority of community outreach initiatives.

I recommend following Christ's plan in Luke 10:1-12 to begin neighborhood evangelism before starting these kind of outreach programs.

The New Testament's chronology of Jesus' ministry shows that He sent out His seventy-two disciples, as described in this passage, for a time period of less than three months. Embarking on an evangelism project lasting in the inner city for about the same length of time creates needed momentum when starting a new initiative. Churches should accomplish the following tasks to launch the project:

1. Mobilize Leadership. The Luke 10 Project provides an opportunity for the evangelist to engage the church leaders in discussions about their core values and mission. Church leaders should embrace the responsibility to equip and mobilize their congregations to reach the lost in their cities. Evangelists should also ask them to consider the salvation of the inner city poor as a core value. An outcome of this discussion should be a commitment by the leadership to spearhead, by example, the Luke 10 evangelistic effort.

The pastoral staff members should join the evangelists on at least one prayer walk through the neighborhoods to intercede for the residents. This is a good opportunity to confirm that the Lord is leading them in this outreach. Expect some leaders to feel skeptical at this point and for others to find themselves suddenly under spiritual attack.

Also expect God to work powerfully as you pray. On one such prayer walk, some pastors and I immediately prayed for a wealthy gated condominium community that faced the front of their church. We asked God to provide a Bible study there even though no canvassers could enter it.

Over the next few weeks we stopped and prayed for the same neighborhood whenever we went out the church's door. Amazingly, the Lord used connections between church families and residents in the gated neighborhood to give the senior pastor an opportunity to lead an evangelistic Bible study there.

The church leaders should enlist a project secretary to map and assign routes for the canvassers and to compile results data. Evangelists should focus their energy on recruiting canvassers and Bible study leaders, teaching the equipping class, leading the teams out, conducting evangelistic Bible studies and following up on new believers.

2. Conduct a two-hour training session. The two purposes of the training session are to equip the canvassers and Bible study leaders for their outreaches and to give them the logistic details of the project. To make the training more enjoyable, the leaders "deputize" the participants and let them help teach the session. When participants arrive for the session, the leaders pretend that everyone needs special identification. They use an inkpad to put the participants' thumbprints on a sign-in sheet next to their names and contact information. The facilitator asks everyone to use the "Luke 10 Deputy" title when addressing each other during the training.

Since the equipping information is straightforward, the facilitator divides participants into "buzz groups" and challenges them to become experts on their assigned sections of the training guide. Each group elects a spokesperson to represent them on a panel of experts who sit behind a table in front of the class.

When the group work is done, the facilitator reassembles all the participants and asks the panel members to take turns reading and explaining the instructions from their sections of the training guide. The facilitator adds commentary to drive home important points. After all the sections have been discussed, the facilitator invites participants to join hands in a large circle. Several persons pray to commission the new "deputies."

3. Implement Canvassing. Church leaders announce that they will go out canvassing from a specific date, time and place, rain or shine. This prevents the Evil One from discouraging the team during bad weather. In fact, canvassers should expect bad weather as a test of their resolve and will find God's blessing on their witness when they prevail and press on in the rain.

The Lord gives favor with persons in the neighborhoods as they see the church members' determination to visit them.

For example, when Kim and I recently canvassed during a summer thunderstorm in a public housing neighborhood, five residents agreed to participate in Bible studies. A young single mother expecting her fifth child asked us to pray for her and her boyfriend. Another woman accepted Christ a week later. The Lord made the time there more encouraging by spreading a beautiful rainbow across the sky as the rain stopped. Parents and children came out of their apartments to join us as we enjoyed it.

Our canvassing resulted in an extended network of Bible studies resulting in the salvation of many residents. We sent a van to pick up these families for church. Adults enrolled in our GED outreach and within six months the church began holding cell group meetings in this community.

Sunday afternoons and summer evenings usually are the best times for canvassing. Sunday mornings during the eleven o'clock service are also good opportunities to canvass, especially for churches having earlier services. Canvassers may attend the early service and then meet outside to begin canvassing. Members attending the eleven o'clock service may provide prayer support and childcare for the canvassing teams.

Many unchurched inner city families are home during this time frame, although they may not get up until later in the day. Late weekday mornings and early afternoons are good times to connect with unemployed single mothers while their children attend school or day camps. I usually avoid Saturdays because many families get chores done on this day of the week, although I have seen persons make successful visits then. I often observe Jehovah Witnesses going out early on Saturdays.

Churches located in or near a mixture of neighborhoods that contain different racial and socio-economic demographics have an opportunity to canvass every community and avoid appearing like they are condescendingly singling out the poor.

I suggest using a city map to identify the surrounding neighborhoods of each church location. Members should begin their canvassing at their church's front doors. Then canvassers may say to neighbors that their goal is to invite all the families living within a specified circumference of their church, implying that the church welcomes everyone without discrimination.

The project's secretary should highlight specific street

assignments on copies of a map and hand them out to the teams before they begin canvassing. The teams should be able to follow the maps from the starting out point to their highlighted assigned streets. The secretary and evangelist may need to walk these streets in advance and designate blocks by writing their addresses on the maps. This preparation makes the directions clearer when dividing up long streets or when more than one street is assigned to a team.

Leaders for the Luke 10 Project may mobilize many persons at one time. Large groups may canvass a neighborhood by dividing into groups of four. Each foursome visits in pairs on both sides of an assigned street. For safety, the pairs keep in eye contact distance of each other. They communicate with nearby teams to avoid going to the same doors. The pairs should refrain from entering homes during canvassing to maintain contact with each other. Staying on the doorstep, they offer to visit later if invited in.

At the doors, the canvassers ring or knock only twice and move on if no one answers. They avoid loud authoritative banging usually used by the police. After ringing or knocking they step back from the door so the residents may see them well through the door's peephole or window.

When someone answers the door, one of the Luke 10 evangelists politely introduces the pair and their ministry. During training, we provide an opening statement but encourage the teams to rely on the Holy Spirit's leading for rewording its question. In the spring, a Luke 10 Project team, for example, might use this statement after making introductions: "Would you, or anyone in your household, be interested in a home Bible study about the true meaning of Easter?"

Seeking the "man of peace" described in Luke 10, canvassers should ask about the potential interest of others in the household because the person answering the door might not be the one God had prepared for their invitation. Recently, I invited three adult women while they sat outside of their public housing apartment. They quickly refused our Bible study offer as a teenage son of one of them walked up and began listening to our discussion.

I asked the mother if her son might participate. They started laughing, insinuating that the son behaved too badly to be interested. Defying their negative attitudes towards him, the fifteen-year-old joined in, began attending one of our studies, accepted Christ and brought several friends.

This man of peace principle makes Luke 10 canvassing a relational strategy. Ralph Neighbour's book, *Knocking on Doors, Opening Hearts,* first introduced me to the reality that God still prepares people in neighborhoods as the "man of peace." These people accept the messenger and receive the witness. Through them, the Lord of the harvest reaches their neighbors and others in their circles of influences.

On two of Jesus' evangelism projects, first when He sent out the seventy disciples and then when He sent out His twelve, He instructed them to remain in the homes of the first ones to receive them. This Luke 10 principle works a lot differently from cold turkey, door-to-door evangelism and is the reasoning behind starting ongoing Bible studies after canvassing.

Offering to conduct a Bible study in someone's home, while seeking a man of peace, and inviting their neighbors to the study launches a relational work. Others in the neighborhood who reject the Bible study still fall under the scope of the project because they become impacted by its long-term relational follow-up. Those open to the Gospel receive the witness of the Bible study. Those rejecting the Bible study receive the long-term servant ministries that follow through the man of peace.

I have heard exciting testimonies from persons whom God had prepared for the invitation of canvassers. Last week, a twenty-two-year-old man told me how he had dropped out of high school to spend his teenage years running from state to state with his father who engaged in criminal activities by conning people. Eventually, someone gave him a New Testament at a bus station, which he began reading.

After returning to live with his mother, he found another Bible in her closet. He read a prayer from its cover to become saved and soon came under the conviction that he needed to attend a church. Canvassers knocked on his pubic housing apartment's door minutes after he prayed for this opportunity!

Although I strongly support developing long-term relationships for inner city evangelism, Christ's plan in Luke 10 provides an effective beginning by reaching those whom God has already prepared for the harvest. Finding a "man of peace" provides a foothold for assembling a community of believers in a neighborhood and for meeting other needs. Persons immobilized by fear often underestimate the Lord's ability and faithfulness to prepare the hearts of people to receive His messengers and message.

Canvassers should always approach the many people who sit or stand outside in the neighborhoods, even if they look intimidating. Speaking first to people when passing them shows respect. Not speaking in the inner city usually communicates offensive disrespect. Canvassers should walk up to all who are outdoors, explain the purpose of the visitation and invite them to join a Bible study. Leaving people to guess the canvassers' intentions creates misunderstanding.

Approach men first, before talking to women. By showing men respect canvassers begin building trust and prevent being identified with other strangers who come to the inner city, like police officers, drug addicts, prostitutes' "johns" or homosexuals. Although appreciative of the police, avoid becoming mistaken for them! During canvassing, speak graciously and "keep it real" to begin establishing relationships, asking God to fill you and your co-laborers with His love and goodness to connect with residents.

Leaders give the time and place for teams to meet back after canvassing. Bringing together all the canvassers at the end gives opportunities for testimonies, praise, prayer and for collecting results. Canvassers should keep copies of their own contacts' information. They should personally make sure that these people get followed up on and that the ministry fulfills all promises made to them.

The leaders of the Luke 10 project should also instruct participants to keep good records. For residents who accept an invitation to participate in a home Bible study, the canvassers should write down their names, addresses and phone numbers. They should turn in this information to a designated secretary after the teams reassemble.

4. *Follow up on contacts and lead Bible studies.* Evangelists should recruit leaders for the evangelistic Bible studies. The secretaries should ensure that these Bible study leaders have copies of the outlines, the locations of the host families

and personal data from any other guests. Persons from the canvassing teams make good Bible study leaders because they have already bonded with the new contacts in their neighborhood.

The Luke 10 coordinators ought to call their Bible study leaders during the week to remind them to prepare their lessons and to call their guests.

The Bible study leaders should immediately call the homes of prospective participants to arrange the first meeting. These leaders should remain flexible and expect some to change their plans. Perseverance in spiritual warfare is important during the follow-up phase. The next chapter includes organizing the Bible studies to prepare for the spiritual opposition that comes with this evangelism.

Project Inventory

Check off tasks as your accomplish them when planning
your Luke 10 Project:

__ Mobilize leadership

A. Pastoral Staff Prayer Walk
B. Evangelists
C. Secretary
D. Bible Study

__ Conduct a two-hour training session

__ Implement canvassing

__ Follow up contacts and lead Bible studies

19 | Overcoming Opposition

From when I worked as the youth director at Faith Community Church, I remember Deacon Richard Moore, a senior African-American, quoting church members from his former generation when he announced prayer meetings. He often encouraged those who felt spiritually attacked on meeting nights with this challenge: "As the old folks used to say, 'You have to press your way out!'"

I still quote his admonition to myself and to our staff team when the forces of darkness begin discouraging us from going out into the communities for evangelism. We have to press our way out every time by using the following guidelines:

1. *Anticipate spiritual opposition from the forces of evil.* Feelings of apprehension, hesitancy, hopelessness, uselessness, laziness and depression usually come on the canvassing team as the Evil One tries to prevent God's people from going out. Canvassing teams must pray and press on through these feelings and through distractions, family conflicts, temptations and discouragement, being strong in the Lord and in His mighty power (Ephesians 6).

Here at Urban Discovery Ministries we require our Luke

10 evangelists to recruit twenty prayer partners to intercede for them and their teams. Canvassing on Sunday mornings and Wednesday evenings also provide ready-made prayer partners during the outreach. Team members should email their prayer warriors weekly to remind them to pray.

<u>2. Expect an inward battle with fear that comes with the assignment.</u> Evangelists usually experience intense fear and doubt as they head to the neighborhoods. When this anticipated attack happens to me, I quote Psalm 27:1, "The LORD is my light and my salvation, whom shall I fear? The LORD is the strength of my life; of whom shall I be afraid?" Sometimes when we meet to get started I have to announce, "Let's get off of this spot. Satan would love to have us stand here all night!" Once we move out to the streets, the forces of evil cannot intimidate so easily.

Often when I start out canvassing in a neighborhood, I cross paths with scary-looking people. Many times they turn out to be friends after I approach them. Perhaps our Lord posts them to test our resolve and to show His ability to open doors for us.

This recently occurred when Kim and I began walking towards our targeted apartment building in a public housing neighborhood. I noticed an intimidating young adult male. He leaned on a car parked in front of the same complex that we had intended to visit. I determined to introduce us and our intentions to him before beginning our canvassing.

When I stopped next to him, the young man remarked, "Don't I know you? You took me to camp when I was little." I told him about our purpose and asked him where he lived in the building, hoping that he was our "man of peace."

He replied, "Oh, I don't live here. I was riding through and had a flat tire." Just then, his friends pulled up in another car and he rode off with them.

3. Acquire and Maintain Momentum. One advantage of coaching AAU basketball with quick players is the ability to execute aggressive defensive presses to cause turnovers and steals. I learned that players must acquire and maintain momentum to develop into successful pressing teams. Full and half-court presses must be mastered early in the season, reviewed at almost every practice and utilized in just about every game.

I attempt to end practices with fierce defensive competition that allows my teams time to gain confidence and momentum. Learning to press makes a team vulnerable at the beginning of the season as its players risk failure while mastering the dynamics involved.

This process mirrors the momentum that evangelists must achieve when pressing their way out to witness for Christ. Getting off of square one becomes the greatest challenge because Satan attempts to immobilize Christians who try to begin. He will tempt well-meaning believers to make the process so complicated that no one moves. I advise keeping the plan simple, go out immediately and keep up the momentum by going out as often as possible.

Leaders should plan their strategies and pray while already in the community sharing the gospel. Like ships that steer easier when moving, leaders should start with simple strategies, since unsaved families crave relationships more than entertaining programs. I advise ministries to make gaining momentum one of their first priorities.

4. *Prepare logistics for the Bible studies ahead of time to start off well.* Set the times and place with the host family of the upcoming Bible studies and communicate with them and the other guests again by phone or through a visit during the week prior to the study. Bringing sodas, a nice dip with crackers or a dessert to start off is often a good way to break the ice. During the refreshments, the leader should ask permission to move chairs so that everyone sits in a circle. Then the leader can politely move the guests into the proper room and begin the Bible study with a prayer.

Leaders should also observe ways to serve the families during the week, make sure everyone knows the details of the next meeting and keep good records of names, addresses and phone numbers. Unless the Spirit leads otherwise, leaders should end the first meeting on time.

5. Keep prayer a vital part of the Bible Studies. Besides enlisting twenty prayer partners to intercede before, during and after the study, team members should pray silently throughout each lesson. In addition, the leader should ask for prayer requests at the close of each study and invite the group to participate in a voluntary, optional prayer time. The Lord's answers to these prayers become an important part of a team's witness to the unbelievers.

6. *Focus on Jesus' work on the cross.* Emphasize God's

holiness and our need for a Savior to pay the punishment of death for our sins and to reconcile us to God. Explain how Jesus died as our substitute and rose again. The team should take every opportunity to exalt Jesus as God, Savior, Christ and King. They may express their love and faith in Christ as they worship before the other participants. I designed the Luke 10 evangelistic Bible study outlines given in the next chapter to provide these opportunities to focus on the cross and exalt the Lord.

7. *Work together to prevent interruptions.* Especially when the group discusses Christ's work on the cross, expect the forces of evil to attempt to distract from the most critical part of the Gospel. Knowing that these attacks come, those not presenting the Gospel should stay prayerfully poised to deflect distractions that hinder a clear understanding of Christ's sacrifice on the cross. Team members may have to pick up and comfort crying children and ask permission to move potential distractions to another room or outdoors to prevent interruptions.

8. *Remain flexible while seeking to continue the studies.* The evangelistic Bible studies in Chapter 20 begin in Genesis and transition into the Christmas and Easter stories. The Luke 10 teams should expect the Lord to provide different kinds of opportunities with each Bible study scheduled. Some residents may desire only one meeting and the leader should prayerfully select the appropriate lesson for it. Other Bible study groups may finish all the lessons and grow into long-term discipleship or church planting ministries.

Leaders should remain flexible while seeking to continue their studies until God saves persons and brings them into a church cell ministry. Every lesson emphasizes a particular truth from the Gospel and provides opportunities to expand the presentation and to bring persons to the Lord. During meetings expect the Spirit of God to change the lesson plans.

9. *Begin the project quickly.* The provided lesson outlines give Luke 10 teams the opportunity to rapidly launch relational inner city evangelism. I recommend beginning without long training sessions and committee meetings. One training class should suffice to mobilize teams. Churches may vary the number of participants. They may challenge their entire congregations to participate in one-time or seasonal projects and select smaller teams to canvass year-round. A combination of both strategies gives the best results.

10. *Use seasonal opportunities.* During summers, consider launching the Luke 10 Project for adults while conducting neighborhood Bible clubs for their children. At UDM, we have sent Christian teenagers to Child Evangelism Fellowship's overnight June training camps. They become quickly equipped at these affordable camps with the know-how and materials to teach the inner city children's clubs. Recruit children for these one-week clubs while canvassing for the adult Bible studies. Conduct these children's clubs at recreation centers, in backyards, on porches, in kitchens, along sidewalks or at places with shade in their neighborhoods.

Outdoor summer clubs scheduled in evenings, after the heat breaks, often work best because many children stay out late at night and sleep in during the mornings or go to day camps. Make special follow-up visits to the parents of children who respond to the Gospel.

Canvassers may also recruit children for church summer camps by establishing a spring scholarship fund to help make them affordable. We began planting our first congregation with these three neighborhood outreaches that jump-started our relational evangelism: Bible studies, children's clubs and summer camps. To keep relational evangelism the priority, make these outreaches as simple as possible by partnering with other ministries that specialize in the camps and clubs. For example, we partner with the Fellowship of Christian Athletes and send young people to their sports camps.

11. Address other needs once relationships become well established. The Luke 10 Project makes the outreach family and community-based. Churches should avoid trying to set up comprehensive mercy programs at the beginning. Wait until after the relational evangelism becomes strong before trying to network with other programs and agencies. Program-based service organizations may immobilize your teams with meetings and questions before people from your ministry make their first visit to an inner city neighborhood.

Learn from the community how to "hang" with them before trying to bring changes. People in the inner city have seen many programs come and go. Relationships of trust take time to develop but give the best results.

12. Respect the Lord's determination to thrust out laborers. Scripture gives many examples of times when the Lord used difficult circumstances to press men and women into His service. His interventions in the lives of Job, Jacob, Ruth, Esther, Jonah and Paul are well known. I minister in the inner city because the Lord broke me through discipline and then redirected my path several times. The complete story of how the Lord thrust me into this type of ministry is detailed in my first book, *Reconciling an Oppressor.*

The Lord of the Harvest's intrusion into the lives of His witnesses resembles a tactic of 18th century British ship captains. Prior to the Revolutionary War, Virginia's governor authorized these captains to draft needed crew members from among Norfolk's unwilling colonists. The captains often organized "press gangs" that raided taverns to kidnap unsuspecting, intoxicated young men and press them into service.

The raiders usually hit these men on the back of their heads with wooden pins and then carried them onto the ships. By the time the captives regained consciousness, they were far from shore with the choice of remaining in chains or working for the captains during the voyages. Most spent several years in England before earning passage back to the colonies.[1]

I know from many experiences that evangelicals should not underestimate the Lord of the Harvest's commitment to respond to the prayer for laborers in the inner city. Believers, at the least, should express and demonstrate to the Lord their willingness to go there. Before becoming inebriated by quests for peace and prosperity in this life, which neglect the inner city harvest, Christians should wisely admonish one another to acknowledge the "wooden pins" that our Lord might use to press out laborers and make His harvest happen. "I know that the LORD secures justice for the poor and upholds the cause of the needy" (Psalm 140:12 NIV).

Press Inventory

1. Evaluate your progress in these areas:

__ Anticipate spiritual opposition from the forces of evil.

__ Expect an inward battle with fear that comes with the assignment.

__ Acquire and maintain momentum.

__ Prepare logistics for the Bible studies ahead of time to start off well.

__ Keep prayer a vital part of the Bible studies.

__ Work together to prevent interruptions.

__ Remain flexible while seeking to continue the studies.

__ Begin the project quickly.

__ Use seasonal opportunities.

__ Address other needs once relationships become well established.

2. In what ways have you experienced being thrust into the inner city harvest?

3. Action Step: Recruit twenty prayer partners for the Luke 10 Project.

20 | Leading Outreach Studies

Lesson One: God's Purpose for Mankind

<u>Objectives</u>:
To introduce the Bible as the inspired Word of God.
To introduce the theme of the Bible: salvation through faith in Jesus Christ.

<u>Lesson Outline</u>:
"For this study, let's assume that the Bible is what it claims to be and see what happens"

I. The Bible's claims in 2 Timothy 3:15-16 and 2 Peter 1:21-22:

A. "What makes the Bible different from any other book?"
   [The Bible is God-breathed. God "breathed" His words through men who wrote them down. Although God did not override their personalities or writing styles, He supernaturally inspired their words and grammar. The original writings came from God with no errors making the Bible trustworthy and the authority for what we believe and do. Every part of the Bible has one interpretation so we seek to understand what God intended for the words to mean when He gave them. There are also many ways to apply the Bible's lessons to our lives.]

B. Consider this logic:
   If God is love and just then He would:
   1. Communicate with mankind (Revelation).

2. Write down His message to make it universal
   (Inspiration).
3. Preserve it through the generations (Preservation).
4. Make His message come alive in our hearts as we
   read or hear it (Illumination).

II. The Bible's Table of Contents: The Bible is made up of 66
books that we may arrange in sections. Mark these sections in
your Bible's Table of Contents:

    A. Old Testament

Law	Genesis – Deuteronomy
History	Joshua – II Chronicles
Poetry	Job – Song of Songs
Major Prophets	Isaiah – Daniel
Minor Prophets	Hosea – Malachi

    B. New Testament

Gospels	Matthew-John
History	Acts
Paul's Letters	Romans – Philemon
General Letters	Hebrews – Jude
Prophecy	Revelation

    C. Practice finding these sections by "cutting" the Bible like a
        deck of cards:
        1. Open the Bible halfway and where do you land?
           [Poetry (usually the book of Psalms)]
        2. Cut the front half in its middle and where do you land?
           [History]
        3. Cut this first front part in its middle and where do you
           land? [Law]

4. Open at the beginning and where do you land? **[Genesis]**
5. Cut the second half of the Bible in its middle and where do you land? **[Gospels]**
6. Cut the back half in its middle and where do you land? **[Paul's Letters]**
7. Cut the last half in its middle and where do you land? **[General Letters]**
8. Open at the end and where do you land? **[Revelation]**

III. Chapter and Verses

A. Demonstrate how to find chapters and verses in the Bible using references from Genesis 1.

B. Optional Activity:

Reinforce this understanding by playing a "Sword Drill" game using these verses:

Joshua 1:8

Psalm 119:11

Matthew 7:24

James 1:25

Sword Drill is a fun game where the study's participants race against each other to find verses in the Bible. The leader says, "Draw your swords!" and then calls out one Bible verse reference while each person holds a Bible by its binding above his or her head. The study members say the verse's reference together. After a short pause the leader then says: "Charge!" At this command, the participants race each other to see who can be the first one to find and read the verse. The first person to begin reading the verse wins a point. The group repeats this competition using a different verse each time.

Lesson Two: The Trinity

<u>Objectives</u>: To introduce the Trinity through creation.

To introduce the purposes of God for His people.

<u>Lesson Outline</u>:

I. Genesis 1:1

"In the beginning God created the heavens and the earth . . ."

A. What role did God the Son, Jesus Christ, have in creation? John 1:1-3; Hebrews 1:2,3

[Spoke creation into existence; took action on the Father's behalf to accomplish the Father's will]

B. What role did the Holy Spirit have in creation? Genesis 1:2 **[Prepared the earth for creation]**

C. What role did God the Father have in creation? Hebrews 1:2 **[Made the universe through the Son]**
[Comparing Genesis 1:1 with these verses shows that God is one with three distinctions: God the Father, God the Son (Jesus Christ) and God the Holy Spirit – all made of the same divine stuff.]

II. Eternity Past: Romans 8:28-30

A. When did God establish His purposes for His people? **[Before creation God gave His people the destiny of becoming like Jesus Christ. Draw a time-line with arrows to show eternity before creation and after the Second Coming of Christ. Explain how God is all-knowing and sees eternity in a glance.]**

B. In eternity past, God implemented a plan to rescue His people from the consequences of their sin through the sacrificial death of Jesus Christ. **[Explain the Gospel in detail and give an invitation if the door opens here]**. This plan of salvation unfolds throughout the Bible.

Lesson Three: The Lord's Authority

Objective: To proclaim that Jesus is God, our risen Lord, and that we must surrender control of our lives to Him

Lesson Outline:

I. Who is in charge?

Is God in charge and we follow Him or are we in charge and God follows us?

[Explain two opposing world views: One where man makes himself the center of the universe and wants everything to revolve around him versus the belief that God rules the universe and we should submit to His authority.]

II. From Genesis 2

Let's discover from the Bible who is in charge:

V. 7	Who made whom?
V. 8	Who decided where man would live?
V. 9	Who gave man the responsibility to work?
V. 15–17	Who established the rules?
V. 17	Who decreed the consequences for sin?
V. 18	Who decided that man needed a helper?
V. 21-22	Who decided to create woman from man's rib?
V. 23-24	Who established marriage?

III. From Ephesians 5:22-32

What does marriage illustrate about our relationship with our Lord? [Our relationship with Jesus, our risen Lord, is illustrated when the husband gives himself sacrificially for his wife. Explain at this point the work of Christ on the cross, His resurrection and His exaltation as Lord. Emphasize how we honor Him by submitting to His authority like the wife is supposed to honor her husband. Also, the Lord will not allow sex outside of marriage because it defiles this illustration.]

From Romans 10:9,10

[Explain from these verses that one must confess and believe that Jesus is God - the risen LORD of the Bible - to be rescued from God's punishment of sin. Believing that Jesus is God requires turning control of one's life over to Him.]

Invitation:

Do you want to surrender control of your life to the Risen Savior, Jesus Christ the Lord?

Do you believe that Jesus is God who died on the cross to pay for the punishment for your sins?

Are you willing to turn from sin and give control of your life to Jesus?

[Be prepared to explain the John 3:16 gospel diagram on an individual basis.]

Lesson Four: The Need for a Deliverer

Objectives: To show the consequences of sin.
              To explain the purpose for Jesus death on the
              cross.
              To present the gospel through His promise of a
              deliverer in Genesis 3:15.

Lesson Outline: Genesis 3

I. Introduction Question:

"If God knew that Satan would rebel and then deceive Eve,
why did He create Satan in the first place?" [As a test of obedience for mankind – God did not want robots so He gave man the freedom of choice.]

II. Read Genesis 3:1-6

A. Satan's deceptions:

In what ways did Satan deceive Eve?

3:1   Distorted and raise doubts about God's Word.

3:4   Lied that there are no consequences for
       disobedience.

3:4   Lied that sin does not bring the punishment of death.
       [Denied that God is holy and just and must carry out the
       punishment of death that He had decreed.]

3:4   Defamed God's character and holiness.

3:4   Offered Eve the opportunity to be like God.

B. Eve's response:

3:6   When should have Eve resisted the temptation?
        [When she first looked upon the fruit]
        What was the difference between Eve and Adam's
        response? [Eve was deceived, Adam chose to disobey]

C. God's Promise:

3:15   Jesus died on the cross as our substitute to satisfy
        God's holy punishment of sin. In 3:15, is the word
        "offspring" singular or plural?
        [Show from the verse that it is singular and how this indicates
        the promise of a Savior. This verse is the first promise in the
        Bible of the Deliverer who will crush Satan's head.]

D. Question:

How will Satan strike the Deliverer's heel? [Explain the
purpose of Jesus dying on the cross to satisfy God's justice.]

E.. God's Provision as His Plan of Salvation Begins:

3:21   What is significant about the clothing that the Lord
        God provided?
        [The skins required the shedding of the animals' blood. (I use
        here the saying, "anywhere you cut the Bible it bleeds," to
        emphasize how God illustrates throughout the Bible that
        forgiveness comes through the shedding of blood. These
        illustrations point to God's provision of salvation through Jesus'
        sacrificial death on the cross.) Explain how sin was passed down
        from Adam through the generations. We not only commit sins,
        but we inherited a sinful nature from Adam. Jesus died on the
        cross as our substitute to satisfy God's justice and pay the
        penalty of death for our sins so that we may receive forgiveness
        and eternal life.]

3:24   Why was God merciful by putting Adam and Eve out
of the garden? **[By keeping them from the Tree of Life,
death allowed them to escape a world cursed by sin and to live
forever with Him in heaven.]**

Invitation:

Since Jesus Christ gave His life for you, will you give your life to
Him? After Jesus humbled Himself to die on the cross for us,
God raised Him from the dead and exalted Him to the highest
place. God decreed that anyone who believes in Jesus will be
given eternal life. Would you receive this gift of eternal life
now? **[Be prepared to explain the John 3:16 diagram that Touch Outreach
Ministries provides.]**

Lesson Five: Three Examples of Unbelievers

<u>Objectives</u>:   To warn against trusting in good works for
salvation.
To warn against rebellion and disregard of God's
means of salvation.
To warn against pride and seeking significance
apart from God.

<u>Lesson Outline</u>:
Three Examples of Unbelievers Whom God Punished

I. Opening Question: What was the best warning that your parents ever gave you?

II. Those who try to trust in their own ways and works to earn God's acceptance:
    A. Cain versus Abel Genesis 4:1–12
    B. Why did God accept Abel's sacrifice and not Cain's?
      [Compare these verses with Hebrew 11:4. Abel offered his sacrifice
      through faith; Cain depended on himself; perhaps God desired the
      blood sacrifice.]

III. Those who reject God's warnings about judgment:
    Gen 6:1-8
    A. Compare with Hebrews 11:7 and 2 Peter 2:5
    B. Explain God's grace (favor) in Genesis 6:8
    C. How many of each kind of animal went into the ark?
      [Genesis 7:2. The answer depends on what kind of animals. The Lord
      commanded Noah to take seven of the clean animals to have enough
      for blood sacrifices and still not wipe out their kind. Emphasize the
      reason for shedding of blood to illustrate the atoning sacrifice of
      Jesus.]

IV. Those whose aim is to make a name for themselves:

Gen. 11:1-9

How is the aim of the tower builders similar to persons who try to feel significant through their own accomplishments?

Invitation:

Explain Ephesians 2:8-9 and review the Gospel message emphasizing salvation by grace alone through faith in Jesus Christ. Identify some of the good works that many persons trust for salvation. Challenge persons to repent of trusting in their own performance to earn God's acceptance.

Lesson Six: God's Great Promises

<u>Objective</u>:   To present God's plan of salvation as it unfolds
through His promises in the Old Testament

<u>Lesson Outline</u>:

I. Overview of Genesis: Genesis may be divided into two
sections:

Chapters 1-11   Four Main Events
Chapters 11-50   Four Main Men

II. God's Plan of Salvation. God's plan of salvation begins
unfolding in the Old Testament as He makes promises to
Abraham in Genesis:

A. The Lord first chooses a man (Abraham) and establishes a
covenant promising him a great nation and the Savior.

B. The Lord introduces to Abraham the order of Kings/Priests
from which the Savior will come.

C. Through Abraham, the Lord chooses a family to whom He
passes on His promises.

D. Through this family, God chooses a nation as His people
- the Nation of Israel - and establishes a covenant with
them through Moses.

E. Through this nation, the Lord establishes a Kingdom
through a covenant with King David, on whose throne
Jesus our Savior will reign.

III. God's Promises to Abraham:

Genesis 12:1-2: From our previous studies, how does the
LORD bless all the peoples on the earth through Abraham?
(Review the Gospel)

IV. The King/Priest Order of Melchizedek: Genesis 14:17-20

A. How did Melchizedek illustrate the coming Lord Jesus Christ? [Melchizedek and Jesus both have the combined offices of King and Priest, both are priests in the greatest priesthood, both are kings of Jerusalem and both used bread and wine in their ministries.]

B. How is Jesus both King and High Priest today? [He is exalted in heaven as our Lord and as our High Priest who intercedes for us. This is why we pray in Jesus' name.]

V. Jesus Promised that He Will Come Again as King: Rev. 22:20

Invitation:

Quote John 14:6 and challenge persons to put their trust in Jesus as the only way to come to God and receive eternal life.

Lesson Seven: Anticipation Is the Best Part!

<u>Objectives</u>:   To give the pieces of the puzzle so we may
appreciate why Christmas is so special.
To emphasize God's holiness and our need for
a Savior.
To show God's love and mercy.
To emphasize the deity of Christ.
To explain that salvation is a free gift.

<u>Lesson Outline</u>:

I. Opening Question: "Who can share a childhood memory of Christmas Eve anticipation."

II. Joseph and Mary Luke 1:26-38 and Matthew 1:18-25
   A. How do you think Joseph and Mary felt while anticipating this first Christmas?
   B. Why did the angel tell Joseph to name the child Jesus?
   C. To understand the anticipation they felt, let's take a short journey through the Bible to see why this promise of a Savior is needed.

II. God's Deliverer Anticipated Genesis. 2:15-17 and 3:15
God is holy and must punish sin – decreed death.

III. God's Promise Anticipated Genesis 12:1-4
The Lord chooses Abraham and the nation of Israel through whom this Deliverer is promised.

IV. God's Kingdom Anticipated: Isaiah 7:14 and Isaiah 9:6-7
   A. The Lord chooses King David's throne on which this Deliverer will reign as King.

B. Do you think Mary and Joseph's Jewish heritage increased their sense of anticipation for the Christ?

V. Conclusion:

Summarize the angel's Good News to Mary and Joseph. Jesus is:

A. Holy

B. Born of a Virgin

C. The Son of God – explain briefly the Trinity

D. The King who will reign forever

E. Immanuel meaning "God with us"

F. Our Savior who was born to take the punishment for our sins and who now is our risen King

G. Our Way to God and Eternal Life (Romans 6:23)

Invitation: Receive the free gift of salvation.

Lesson Eight: Good News for All Men

<u>Objectives</u>: To present the plan of salvation in clear terms
To exalt Jesus as Savior, Christ and Lord

<u>Lesson Outline</u>: Read Luke 2:1-20

I. Opening Question When did Christmas first become more than a holiday to you?

II. The Angels Announce Good News to Shepherds
   A. The Old Testament (Micah 5:2) prophesied that the Christ would be born in Bethlehem.
   B. What did God do in history to fulfill this prophecy?
   C. What would you do if an angel appeared to you with a message about God's plan for your life?
   D. Who sent the angel with a message?
   E. For whom was the angel's message intended?
   F. What was the angel's news?
   G. How did the angel's message describe Jesus?
   [Explain Jesus as Savior, Christ, Lord and present the plan of salvation and the deity of Christ in simple terms:
   Savior – Jesus died on the cross to pay the punishment of death for sin.
   Christ – Jesus anointed as King.
   Lord   – Jesus is God.]

III. Good News For All People
Compare this passage with John 3:16. Why did the angel say that the message was "good news" of great joy for all people?

<u>Invitation</u>: Invite the participants to rejoice in this good news and receive the Lord Jesus Christ as their Savior, God and King.

Lesson Nine: How to Meet the Christ

<u>Objectives</u>:
> To review God's plan of salvation.
> To proclaim repentance, challenging participants
> to surrender control of their lives to the Lord Jesus.
> To invite participants to believe in Jesus and to
> receive Him as their Savior, God and King.
> To emphasize that salvation is by grace through faith.

<u>Lesson Outline</u>: Read Matthew 2:1-18

I. Opening Question. Give thanks for one way that our study of the Bible has made Christmas more meaningful to you.

II. The Christmas Story

A. Who missed the coming of the Christ? **[Roman Emperor, King Herod, religious leaders]**

B. Why do you think the news of the birth of Christ, the King of the Jews, disturbed Herod and the religious leaders?
[Pride and wanting to control their own lives, rebellion against God's word, trusting self-righteousness, no sorrow for sin and unwillingness to submit to the Christ (repentance).]

C. Compare this passage with John 1:11,12. How did the magi (often called kings) receive Jesus?
[Explain the Gospel using John 1:12 – emphasizing the Name of the Lord Jesus Christ to proclaim Him as God, Savior, and King.]

<u>Invitation</u>: Challenge participants to turn over control of their lives to Jesus and to trust Him alone for salvation.

Lesson Ten: Mission Accomplished!

Objective: To proclaim Jesus as the risen Christ, emphasizing
His work of salvation on the cross.

Lesson Outline: Read Luke 23:26 - 24:8

I. Opening Question. "What was your biggest school or career
assignment?"

II. Jesus' Mission
In what ways do these verses show that Jesus fulfilled a mission,
as the Christ, through His death and resurrection?

III. Jesus' Ministers to a Thief Read Luke 23:32-49
  A. Note that thief on the cross called out to the Lord and
      received forgiveness and eternal life by believing in Jesus.
  B. Emphasize that the thief did not deserve salvation nor
      could he do anything to earn it.
  C. Emphasize that salvation is a free gift and is not earned by
      going to church or by being baptized. One must trust
      Jesus' work on the cross to get to paradise, not by trusting
      one's own accomplishments.
  D. Point out the sorrow for sin that the thief demonstrated
      and how he surrendered control of his life to Jesus as God,
      which defines repentance.

IV. Angels Testify about Jesus' Resurrection Read Luke 24:1-8
  A. They testified that Jesus has risen.
  B. They explain that Jesus had to be delivered to sinful men,
      crucified and on the third day be raised from the dead.

C. Compare with 1 Peter 2:21-25. Ask: What was the
reason that the Christ had to die for us?
Explain the holiness of God and how Jesus died as our
substitute to pay the punishment of death for our sins.
D. According to Romans 10:9-13, what should be our
response to the news that Jesus is the risen Lord?

[These verses challenge us to believe in the deity of Jesus Christ as the
risen Lord and to trust in Him for forgiveness and for salvation from
God's punishment of our sins. Explain that everyone must, at a certain point in his or her life, realize the need to be rescued from the
punishment from sin, believe in Jesus as the risen Lord who died to
pay this punishment and trust Him for salvation.]

Invitation:
Who is willing to call on our risen Jesus Christ to receive eternal
life, like the thief did on the cross?

Appendix

Correcting Systemic Injustices
in Evangelical Structures

Action in One's Personal Life

Take initiative to enter the inner city harvest in spite of fears.

Begin crossing racial, economic, educational and culture divides even when these moves impose on lifestyles and require personal sacrifices.

Take initiatives to respond in measurable ways to Christian leaders who call for crossing these divides.

Choose to support outreaches based on their effectiveness in discipleship and not for their emotional appeal or their potential marketability.

Establish accountability to budget time for developing evangelistic relationships (budget at least three hours per week).

Pass on relationship-based justice and mercy values to children to embed these values deeper into evangelical thinking.

Action for Churches

Free members from building-centered programs that limit time and accessibility for evangelism and that detract from extending true mercy to the poor.

Confront and reject homogeneous church growth strategies that discriminate against the inner city poor.

Locate ministries to strategically connect with the poor.

Accept local church responsibility for ministry to families from low-income backgrounds.

Put mercy, justice and the inner city poor high on church leadership agendas.

Measure church program effectiveness by the way they mobilize members for relationship-based mercy and justice.

Limit or restructure event and program-based evangelism strategies that neglect the poor.

Help to end the racial divide among churches through evangelism and empowerment.

Empower local church evangelists in your church to mobilize members for relationship evangelism.

Choose lasting, relational discipleship ministries in the inner city with families rather than temporary, convenient projects that might make helpers feel merciful but may actually enable irresponsible behavior.

Embrace strategies for mobilizing African-Americans for world missions and for creating racially diverse evangelism teams in the states.

Empower black leaders to govern instead of trusting in multi-cultural music alone to create diversity in churches.

Exalt mercy and justice as qualifications for accomplishing God's purposes.

Repent of moral compromise, materialism and politics by church leaders, which alienate inner city men from Christianity.

Evangelize inner city neighborhoods through mercy relationships and by confronting injustices.

Expose the genocide of aborting unborn black babies for economic or any other reasons.

Repent of letting white nostalgia prevent the integration of church leadership.

Mobilize for relational inner city ministry because the harvest is ready.

Pray diligently for inner city laborers.

Repent of the middle-class survivor mentality that causes flight from the inner city.

Refuse to follow the patterns of neglect maintained by many middle-class white churches.

Correctly handle 10/40 Window strategies while pursuing responsibilities to serve the local poor.

Organize diverse missions teams and movements by partnering with ministries that empower leaders from the inner city to prevent Satan from discrediting the true Gospel of Jesus Christ.

Action in Education

Include ministry to the poor in Christian school boards' mission statements.

Mobilize the body of Christ to solve the educational crisis in the inner city.

Call evangelical Christians to work or volunteer in public school systems while overcoming financial barriers to provide Christian education for inner city children.

Action in Leadership Development

Empower inner city men as leaders.

Minister to inner city men to prevent their incarceration, not just during their incarceration.

Use the influence of women who are connecting with inner city women and children to recruit and mobilize Christian men to reach inner city men.

Partner with mature ministries that empower inner city leaders to prevent Christian paternalism that offends and cripples inner city residents and promotes dependency.

Action in Racial Reconciliation

Increase the awareness of the devastating spiritual consequences of segregation and take steps to cross the divide.

Openly address segregation and resolve past offenses at evangelical Bible colleges and seminaries while defending evangelical doctrine in the inner city.

Include justice and mercy in the mission statements and curricula of evangelical Bible colleges and seminaries. Expand their philosophies to also include bringing biblical scholarship to the inner city, equipping workers for the inner city harvest (and not just the middle class) and mobilizing persons of African descent for world missions.

Glossary of Author's Definitions

Abolitionists. People who want to end slavery and the slave trade. Participants in a large political movement called abolitionism that started in the mid 1700's.

American Athletic Union. P.O. Box 22409, Lake Buena Visa FL 32830. (800)AAU-4USA. Website: http://aausports.org.

American Dream. The aspiration that hard work will bring prosperity and give children better lives than their parents.

Assimilation. The process of losing cultural differences when becoming absorbed by a larger cultural group.

Believers. Christians who put their faith in the Lord Jesus Christ alone for salvation.

Biblical Authority. The theological presupposition that the Bible is the authority for every thing that one believes and practices.

Biblical Infallibility. The theological presupposition that the Bible is completely trustworthy.

Black Experience. Describes a common awareness in people of African ancestry from their history and culture. It includes unique circumstances, beliefs, viewpoints and expressions in the modern world created by the struggle for freedom from oppressive economic, social, and political forces.

Black Theology. A theology of liberation founded on a belief that the black experience is equal to or greater than the authority of the Bible.

Black Power. A word introduced in the 1960's by Stokley

Carmichael of the Black Panthers, which now describes African-Americans' positive aspirations for self-reliance, self-liberation and national self-determination (government).

Book of Life. A book in heaven that records the names of those who receive eternal life through faith in Jesus Christ.

Born Again. The phrase comes from Jesus in John 3:3, 7 where He tells Nicodemus that he must be born again to enter the God's kingdom. Jesus explains that this new, second birth is a spiritual work accomplished by the Holy Spirit (called regeneration) in people when they put their faith in Jesus.

Brown versus Board of Education of Topeka. The 1954 U.S. Supreme Court landmark case that outlawed racial segregation in public education facilities by ruling against the "separate but equal" doctrine.

Civil Rights Movement. The organized struggle to achieve, by non-violent protests, national equal rights legislation for African Americans.

Child Evangelism Fellowship. P.O. Box 348, Warrenton MO 63383. (636) 456-4321. Website: www.cefonline.com.

Christian Education. Education in the home, church or school from the Christian perspective that integrates biblical principles into every subject area.

Christian School Movement. The worldwide growth in numbers of evangelical and fundamental protestant Christian schools since the 1960's.

Core Values. Lasting, indispensable and fundamental values that guide an organization's priorities, decision-making and actions.

Cultural Diversity. Having a variety of groups in an organization or a geographical area from different racial or ethnic backgrounds, social structures, perspectives, values, styles and expressions, etc. Emphasizes the freedom to be culturally different without needing to conform to another culture to feel valued, accepted or successful.

Discipleship. Teaching/mentoring, which Jesus Christ demonstrated, commanded and promised to empower, including baptizing and providing accountability for obedience to Him (Matthew 28:18-20).

Educational Therapy. Direct and individualized instruction developed by the National Institute for Learning Disabilities to stimulate cognitive and perceptual function for students with learning disabilities.

Ethnocentrism. To feel that one's own culture is superior to others and to measure other cultures by one's own.

Enabling Behavior. When someone plays a role in helping another person continue in destructive behavior by removing consequences or by provocation.

Environment. Used in this book to describe the changing external conditions and circumstances that impact inner city ministry and affect the kinds of evangelism strategies and methodologies required for successful outreach.

Evangelical. In this book this word identifies Christians who hold the conservative doctrines of traditional evangelicalism, which include the infallibility, inerrancy and authority of the Bible. A few of the other doctrines essential to evangelicalism are the deity, virgin birth, substitutionary atonement, resurrection and certain return of Jesus Christ. These Christians also believe that Jesus commissioned them to proclaim His Gospel throughout the world and thereby make for Him disciples from every ethnic group.

Evangelist. From Ephesians 4:11, this book uses this word to describe spiritual gifted persons given by Christ to prepare God's people for the work of evangelism in various forms.

Fellowship of Christian Athletes (FCA). 8701 Leeds Road, Kansas City, MO 64129. (800)289-0909. Website: www.fca.org.

Fundamentalism. Positively named for the set of "fundamental" doctrines that conservative evangelical Christians defended when taking a stand against liberalism around the turn of the 20th century. By the mid-20th century, the movement had begun emphasizing religious separatism as a biblical mandate. This emphasis on separatism is a primary difference between fundamentalism and traditional, conservative evangelicalism.

Gentrification. When redevelopment of an inner city neighborhood raises its property values so that housing there becomes unaffordable to residents with low-incomes. The poor must move elsewhere as more affluent residents replace and/or displace them.

Ghettoize. Refers to the phenomena of restricting the poor and those who call for mercy on their behalf to secluded geographical areas, causes or charitable organizations for the purposes of isolating and protecting one's lifestyle from change, sacrifice or obligation - the opposite of extending true mercy.

Gospel. "Moreover, brethren, I declared unto you the Gospel which I preached unto you, which also ye have received, and wherein you stand . . . by which ye are saved . . . For I delivered unto you first of all that which I also received, how that Christ died for our sins according to the scriptures; and that He was buried, and that He rose again the third day according to the scriptures . . ." (I Corinthians 15:1-4).

Great Commission. "And Jesus came and spake unto them, saying, "All power is given unto Me in heaven and in earth. Go ye therefore, and teach all nations, baptizing them in the name of the Father, and of the Son, and of the Holy Ghost. Teaching them to observe all things whatsoever I have commanded you: and, lo, I am with you always even unto the end of the world (Matthew 28:18-20).

Great Migration. The mass move of African-Americans (1910-1970) to northern and mid-western urban industrial areas from rural life in the South.

Harvest (Spiritual). From Jesus' use of agriculture to explain the work of evangelism in terms of a harvest.

Jim Crow. An era after Reconstruction (beginning in late 1800's) of white oppression in many ways against African-Americans. This oppression occurred mostly in border and southern states and included the enforcement of racial segregation using Jim Crow Laws.

Liberalism. A theological system that rejects the Bible's inerrancy, literal interpretation and authority while allowing evolutionary theories, universalist views about other religions, homosexuality and the development of personal doctrines about God and salvation.

Lost. Jesus' description of those needing to be found by Him whom He came to seek and to save (Luke 19:10).

Man of Peace. In Luke 10: 5-7 Jesus describes with this phrase the residents who would welcome His commissioned evangelists and provide them hospitality. Through the homes of these peace-loving people Christ's evangelists ministered in villages and towns.

Missions. The organized efforts by churches, schools, and/or agencies to recruit, equip, empower, mobilize, manage and support believers for world evangelization for short or long periods of time.

Mobilize. Means in this book's context to organize and prepare God's people to take action in Christ's spiritual harvest.

National Institute for Learning Disabilities (NILD). 107 Seekel Street Norfolk, VA 23505. (877)661-6453. Website: www.nild.net.

Paradigm. A ministry model used as an example or standard.

Park Place School. 509 W. 35th Street, Norfolk, VA 23508. (757)624-3473. Website: www.park-place-school.org.

Paternalism. Refers in this book to disempowering practices, rooted in feelings of superiority, where people take on the responsibility of watching over those less fortunate.

Pie in the Sky. Refers to the concept that the poor should be content with receiving no relief or justice during their poverty on earth by putting their focus on God's eventual rewards for them in heaven. A labor union coined the phrase in 1911 to protest some evangelists' neglect of the poor with this take-off on the hymn *In the Sweet Bye and Bye:*

> **"Long-haired preachers come out every night,**
> **Try to tell you what's wrong and what's right;**
> **But when asked how 'bout something to eat**
> **They will answer with voices so sweet:**
>
> **CHORUS:**
> **You will eat, bye and bye,**
> **In that glorious land above the sky;**
> **Work and pray, live on hay,**
> **You'll get pie in the sky when you die."[1]**

Philosophy. Used in this book to encompass a church, ministry or school's core values, mission and vision in changing spiritual, social, economic, and cultural environments.

Post Modern. Includes, among other contemporary cultural changes, society's present shift towards being more experience orientated, inclusive and community (versus building) centered.

Poverty. Measured in the U.S. by these three indexes (poverty lines): median family income, poverty thresholds, and poverty guidelines. Neighborhoods have poverty rates based on the percentages of residents falling below the poverty lines. Other factors besides income and family size may also increase the financial needs of families and individuals.

Programs. Organized outreach services.

Project Light. P.O. Box 508, Norfolk, Virginia 23501. (757) 624-1764. Website: www.projectlight.org.

Public Housing. Apartments or houses owned and operated by a government authority – usually for people with low incomes.

Racial Discrimination. Treating people unfairly because of race.

Racial Superiority (Feelings of). A mindset that one's race is inherently better than another.

Reconstruction. A time period of rebuilding in the South after the Civil War that had unique political and social developments related to its restoration into the Union and the freedom of former slaves.

Red States. Refers to the thirty-one states that voted Republican in the 2004 election. Television news created the designation of Red and Blue states when reporting the 2000 presidential election results. The colors are now commonly used to identify a cultural divide in America along the political, social and religious differences of conservatives and liberals in these states.

Reformers. Leaders during the Protestant Reformation in the 16th century.

Regeneration. When the Holy Spirit indwells a person and makes his or her dead spirit come alive. This spiritual renewal is referred to as the new birth or being born again.

Relational Evangelism. Introducing persons to Jesus Christ in the context of, and because of, the bond of friendship.

Repentance. Whenever through the Holy Spirit's convicting power a person who is sinning against God responds sorrowfully and becomes willing to turn away from sin and surrender control of his or her life to Jesus Christ.

Sacred Cows. Aspects of a ministry (programs, traditions, policies, etc.) that are exempt from strategic evaluation.

Samaritans. For many historical, religious and racial reasons Jews in Jesus' day considered them inferior and despicable.

Segregation (Racial). The directly imposed and/or institutionalized separation of the races by racial discrimination or by "separate but equal" practices.

Strategic Planning. A prayerful stewardship by leaders who seek the Lord's wisdom for setting a ministry's direction and objectives. Consists of prayer, information gathering, analysis, and long-range goal setting. Leaders seek to preserve core values while moving a ministry towards a future targeted state of outreach under changing environmental conditions.

Structures. In the book refers to the arrangements in churches, ministries and schools that determine the accepted beliefs, cultures, roles, functions and relationships for people going to and coming from the inner city.

TOUCH Outreach Ministries, The Cell Group People. 10055 Regal Row, Suite 180, Houston, TX 77040. (713)896-7478. Website: www.touchusa.org.

Urban Discovery Ministries. P.O. Box 6381 Norfolk, VA 23508. (757)622-1665. Website: www.urbandiscovery.org.

Vision Statement. Communicates the state of existence that the ministry desires to achieve at a specific future date.

Notes

Preface

1 Tobin Miller Shearer, "White Spaces," *The Other Side* (April 2002), 27 Aug. 2004 <http://www.theotherside.org/archive/mar-apr02/shearer.html>.

2 Beverly Daniel Tatum, *"Why Are All the Black Kids Sitting Together in the Cafeteria?"*, (New York: Basic Books, 1997) 94,105.

3 Michael O. Emerson, Christian Smith, *Divided by Faith: Evangelical Religion and the Problem of Race in America* (New York: Oxford University Press, 2000) 132.

Chapter 1

1The U.S. Government defines the inner city as "the older, central part of a city, often characterized by crowded, run-down, low-income neighborhoods." (http:/www.ots.treas.gov/glossary/gloss-i.html). My definition includes these downtown areas and adds the plight of impoverished families living in inner city-type neighborhoods, regardless of where they may be located in relation to the central part of a city. In the Hampton Roads, Virginia, metropolitan area where I live, low-income apartment complexes exist at various locations throughout the cities and impoverished families often reside relatively close to affluent neighborhoods and suburban churches.

2 My definition of the spiritual harvest comes from Jesus' imagery in the Bible and describes the phenomena occurring when God intervenes in the lives of people and reconciles them to Himself. Christ's harvest metaphors include a master, his

laborers, the planting (sowing) of seeds, and the reaping of the wheat. Luke 10 demonstrates how He commissions His disciples as His ambassadors of reconciliation like a master sending out laborers to reap the harvest. Jesus thrusts them out to proclaim His good news to individuals (10:6), families, and communities (10:10-15), which results in God giving spiritual transformation (10:17-19) and eternal life (10:20). Those laboring in this spiritual harvest to gather people to God perform the work of evangelism. Those spiritually gifted by Jesus to equip and lead harvest laborers are evangelists (Eph. 4:11). Those who accept the Bible as the authoritative Word of God that makes this spiritual harvest the purpose of God are evangelicals in the truest sense of the word. Matthew 9:35–10:1; 13:3-9,18-33; 28:18-20; John 4:35-42; Acts 1:8.

[3] "Step 3 – Document Vision, Mission, and Core Values," Strategic IT Planning and Governance: Stage Two, 10 April 2005 <http://www.mcleanreport.com/index.cfm?fuseaction=SITPG_StageTwo&zone=ITS>.

[4] Edward F. Murphy, *Spiritual Gifts and the Great Commission*, (California: Mandate Press, 1975) 259.

[5] Brooks, David. "The New Red-Diaper Babies Make a Family Statement." Editorial. Virginian Pilot 8 Dec. 2004: 24.

[6] "Poll: America's Evangelicals More and More Mainstream but Insecure," Religion & Ethics NewsWeekly, (13 April 2004) 12 Jan 2005 <http://www.pbs.org/wnet.religionandethics/week733/ release.html>.

[7] Emerson and Smith, 166.

[8] "Quotations for Martin Luther King, Jr. Day," Quote Garden, (7 Aug. 2004) 4 Sept. 04 <http://www.quotegarden.com/mlk-day.html>.

9 "Mission – The Rio Grande is a National Boundary, Not an Ecclesial One," North Texas Maryknoll Affiliates, 25 Jan 05 <http://www.teilhard.com/solidarity/workshop14.htm>.

Chapter 2

1 "Step 3 – Document Vision, Mission, and Core Values," McClean Report, InfoTech Research Group, (2 Oct. 2005) <http:// www.infotech.com/MR/SITP/Document%20Business. aspx#>.

2 Guy S. Safford, *Strategic Planning for Christian Organizations*, (Fayetteville, AR: Accrediting Association of Bible Colleges, 1994) 80.

3 "Freestyle Evangelicals: The Surprise Swing Vote," Beliefnet 14 Jan 05 <http://www.beliefnet.com/story/129/story_12995 _2.html>.

4 Anna Greenberg and Jennifer Berktold, "Re: Evangelicals in America," Greenberg Quinlan Rosner Research Inc., (5 April 2004)12 January 05 <http.www.pbs.org/wnet/religionande-thics/week733/ release.html>.

Chapter 3

1 King, "Quotations for Martin Luther King, Jr. Day.

2 C.S. Lewis, *The Screwtape Letters*, (Chicago: Lords and Kings Associates) 34.

3 Leighton Ford, "Jesus the Transforming Leader," Evangelism Leadership Seminar, Leighton Ford Ministries, 14 Sept. 1989.

Chapter 4

1 George Yancy, *One Body One Spirit: Principles of Successful Multiracial Churches*, (Downers Grove: InterVarsity, 2003) 67.

[2] Michael V. Fariss, *Reconciling An Oppressor*, (Washington: Pleasant Word) 117.

Chapter 5

[1] Peter M. Bergman, *The Chronological History of the Negro in America*, (New York: Harper and Row) 10.

[2] Martin Luther King Jr., "Quotations for Martin Luther King, Jr. Day," *Quote Garden*, (7 Aug. 2004) 4 Sept. 04 <http://www.quotegarden.com/mlk-day.html>.

[3] Kim Thoday, "Christianity and the KKK," *John Mark Ministries: Apologetics and Social Issues*, 6 Aug. 2004 <http://www. pastornet.au/JMM/articles/1515.htm>.

[4] Rob Eisinga, Jaak Billiet and Albert Felling, "Christian Religion and Ethnic Prejudice in Cross-National Perspective," *International Journal of Comparative Sociology* (August 1999): v40 i3 375.

[5] Tom Skinner, "The U.S. Racial Crisis and World Evangelism (Urbana 70)," 19 Jan 05 <http://www.urbana.org/_articles.cfm?RecordId=185>.

[6] C. Everett Koop and Francis A. Schaeffer, *Whatever Happened to the Human Race?*, (Westchester: Crossway) 14.

Chapter 6

[1] Hening, ed., The Statutes at Large, vol.2, 260, "Chronology on the History of Slavery 1619 to 1789: 1667/09 – ACT III," 25 Dec. 2003 <http://innercity.org/holt/slavechron.html>.

[2] "Chronology on the History of Slavery and Racism 1830 to the End: 1861," Christopher H. Owen. The Sacred Flame of Love: Methodism and Society in Nineteenth-Century Georgia, Athens and London: The University of Georgia Press, (1998) 25 Dec. 2003 <http://innercity.org/holt/chron_1830_end.html>.

3 Ida B. Wells, *Crusade for Justice: The Autobiography of Ida B. Wells*, (Chicago: University of Chicago, 1970) 111-12.

4 Emerson and Smith, 32-33.

5 "Baptists on the Block," *Christianity Today*, (7 Aug 2000) 21 Jan 05 <http://www.christianitytoday.com/ct/2000/009/12.24.html>.

Chapter 7

1 James H. Cone, *Risks of Faith: The Emergence of a Black Theology of Liberation, 1968-1998*, (Boston: Beacon Press, 1999) Introduction XXII.

Chapter 8

1 "Partisan Politics: Newspaper Opinions," *American Experience/ Times of the Lincolns*, 15 Aug. 2004 <http://pbs.org.wgbh/amex/lincolns/politics/es_media.html>.

2 Gailyn Van Rheenen, "Money and Mi$$ion$ [Revisited]: Combating Paternalism," 24 July 2004 <http://www.guyanna-missions.com/combating_paternalism_GVR.htm>.

Chapter 9

1 "Hampton Roads History and Penny Postcard Tour: Hampton University," *Hampton University History Brief* (6 April 2001) 3 Sept. 2004 <http://www.historichamptonroads.com/HistoryBriefs/hbHamptonUniv.htm>.

2 Francis G. Peabody, *Education for Life, The Story of Hampton Institute*, (Doubleday and Page, 1918) 138-139.

3 Wells, 154-155.

4 Partisan Politics: Newspaper Opinions.

5 Tatum, 83.

Chapter 10

[1] King, "Quotations for Martin Luther King, Jr. Day."

[2] Michael Foust, "Barna: Biblical World View Held by Only Half of Senior Pastors," *LifeWay*, 8 Aug. 2004 <http://www.lifeway.com/lwc/article_main_page/0,1703,A%3D156042%26M%3D50011,00.html>.

[3] James H. Cone, 55.

[4] "Important Philosophical Notes," 7 Aug. 2004 <http://home.CWRU.edu/~ngb2/Pages/ Impor_Phil_Notes.html>.

[5] "Liberal Churches See Drop in Attendance," *Concerned Women for America*, 8 August 2004 <http://www.csfa.org/printerfriendly.asp?id=492&department=cfi&catagoryid=cfreport>

[6] Benton Johnson, Dean R. Hodge, and Donald A. Luidens, "Mainline Churches: The Real Reason for Decline," *First Things*, (1993) 8 Aug. 2004 <http://www.firstthings.com/ftissues/ft9303/johnson.htm>.

[7] Skinner.

[8] Schaeffer, 50-51.

[9] King, "Quotations for Martin Luther King, Jr. Day"

[10] Emerson and Smith, 168.

[11] "Letter From Equal Partners in Faith Concerning the Promise Keepers," Equal Partners in Faith, 16 Jan 05 <http://www.geocities.com/CapitolHill/4497/pk.html>.

[12] "Abortion Surveillance – United States 2001," Morbidity and Mortality Weekly Report (26 Nov 2004) 5 July 2005 <http://www.carnellknowledge.com/pdfs/AbortionRates2001.pdf>.

[13] Phil Johnson, "The Foolishness of Preaching the Gospel," Tape GL PJ-100, 16 Jan 05 <http://www.biblebb.com/files/dobson.htm>.

14 Tom Minnery, *Why You Can't Stay Silent: A Biblical Mandate to Shape Our Culture*, (Wheaton: Tyndale, 2001) 17.

15 Minnery, 141.

16 Minnery, 47.

17 William D. Hungerpiller, *A Tree Planted by the Lord*, (Atlanta, 2001) 33.

18 Elfriede Wedam, "The Mosaic of Black Religion in Indianapolis," *Research Notes Roundtable*, Vol.2, No.8 (Sept. 2000) 21 Aug. 2004 <http://www.polis.iupui.edu/ ruc/newsletters/research.vol2no8.htm>.

19 Wedam, "The Mosaic of Black Religion in Indianapolis."

20 "Abortion and the Black Community," *Life Education and Resource Network*, 4 Sept. 2004 <http://www.blackgenocide. org/black.html>.

21 James Cone, "The Easy Conscience of America's Churches on Race," *CTA Spirituality Justice Reprint*, (2002) <http://www. cta-usa.org>.

22 "Doctrines of the Church of God in Christ" 21 Aug. 2004 <http://www.cogic.org/dctrn.htm>.

23 Corrie Cutrer, "Church of God in Christ: COGIC Presiding Bishop Ousted," *Christianity Today Library.Com*, 8 Sept. 2004 <http:www.ctlibrary.com/6384>.

24 John MacArthur, "Is the Charismatic Movement a Christian Movement?" *Bible Questions and Answers* Part 3 Tape GC 1301-A (1976) 1 Sept. 2004 <http:// www.biblebb.com/files/ maqua/1301-A-14.htm>.

25 "A Glimpse of the Kingdom of Heaven: The Azusa Street Revival," *This Far By Faith: 1864-1945 from Emancipation to Jim Crow*, 7 Aug. 2004 <http://www.pbs.org/thisfarbyfaith/journey_3/p_9.html>.

26 JohnRivera,"Neo-Pentecostalism:Traditional Congregations

Bristle at Stress on the   Individual over Social Activism." The Baltimore Sun, Telegraph, 25 Aug. 2002, A1, 4 July   2005, <http://www.religionnewsblog.com/archives/00000577.html>.

Chapter 11

[1] Bob Sjogren and Gerald Robinson, *Cat and Dog Theology*, (Georgia: Authentic Lifestyle, 2003) 202.

[2] Robert T Coote, "AD 2000" and the '10/40 Window': A Preliminary Assessment," *International Bulletin of Missionary Research*, Oct. 2000 v24 i4, 160.

[3] Fariss, 42.

[4] C.S. Lewis, 43.

[5] "Joshua Project-Peoples by Country Profiles,"11 Jan. <http://www.joshuaproject.net/peopctry.php?rop3=103642&ro g3=HA>.

[6] "Haiti," Global Information Network, Nazarene Missions International, 11 January 2005, <http://www.nazarenemissions.org/education/gin/caribbean/haiti.htm>.

[7] "Haiti Program," Mission Aviation Fellowship, 11 January 05 <http://www.maf.org/services/programs/haiti.html>.

Chapter 12

[1] Rick Warren, *The Purpose-Driven® Life* (Grand Rapids: Zondervan, 2002) 33.

[2] Warren, 237-239.

[3] Frank R. Tillapaugh, *The Church Unleashed*, (Ventura: Regal Books, 1983) 36.

[4] Emerson and Smith, 166.

[5] Frances A. Schaeffer, *A Christian Manifesto*, (Westchester: Crossway Books, 1981) 77.

6 Skinner.

7 Cone, 131,133.

8 John Piper, *The Passion of Jesus Christ* (Wheaton: Crossway, 2004) 12.

9 Piper, 24.

10 Langston, Scott M., "Wresalin' Jacob," *H-Net Review*, 24 July 2004 <http:www.hnet.org/reviews/showrev.cgi?path= 24983967236706>.

Chapter 13

1 Martin Luther King Jr., *Quote DB*, 4 Sept. 2004 <http://www.quotedb.com/quotes/3082>.

2 Warren, 117.

3 Cone, XI.

4 Cone, 12.

5 Martin Luther King, Jr., "Worlds of Quotes.com" 21 December 2003 http://www.worldofquotes.com/author/Martin-Luther-King,-Jr./1/.

6 Cone, 7.

7 Rick Warren, *The Purpose-Driven Church*, (Grand Rapids: Zondervan, 1995) 170.

8 Yancey, 33.

9 Ralph W. Neighbour, *Where Do We Go from Here?*, (Houston: Touch Publications, 2000) 32.

Chapter 14

1 Warren, 281.

2 Skinner.

Chapter 15

[1] Charles C. Ryrie, *The NASV Ryrie Study Bible*, (Chicago: Moody Press, 1978) Note on Hosea 2:18, 1337.

[2] Do not trust in deceptive words and say, "This is the temple of the LORD, the temple of the LORD, the temple of the LORD!" If you really change your ways and actions and deal with each other justly, if you do not oppress the alien, the fatherless, or the widow and do not shed innocent blood in this place, and if you do not follow other gods to your own harm, then I will let you live in this place . . . (Jer. 7:4-7 NIV).

O LORD, Who may dwell in your sanctuary? Who may live on your holy hill? He whose walk is blameless and who does what is righteous. (Ps. 15:1 NIV).

I hate, I despise your religious feasts; I cannot stand your assemblies. Even though you bring home burnt offerings and grain offerings, I will not accept them. Though you bring choice fellowship offerings, I will have no regard for them. Away with the noise of your song! I will not listen to the music of your harps. But let justice roll on like a river, righteousness like a never-failing stream (Amos 5:18-24 NIV).

Is not this the kind of fasting I have chosen, to loose the chains of injustice, and untie the chords of the yoke, to set the oppressed free and break every yoke? Is it not to share your food with the hungry, and to provide the poor wanderer with shelter - when you see the naked, to clothe him, and not to turn away from your own flesh and blood (Is. 58:6 NIV)?

[3] In Genesis 3:15, the LORD confronts Satan who had deceived Eve. With the onslaught of the just consequences of sin, mankind inherited and earned the condemnation of death and alienation from a holy God. Our LORD immediately began to carry out justice on our behalf. By His great covenant mak-

ing mercy, He decrees that the offspring of the woman will crush the head of Satan by sacrificially and subsitutionally atoning for sin. Established in eternity past, God set into motion His plan for our redemption. This redemptive purpose of God forever displays the combined glory of His justice and mercy. The justice of God prevents sinful men from earning a relationship with Him or a place in heaven. Yet the mercy of God compelled Him to send Jesus Christ to pay our debt of death for sin. Jesus substitutionary death perfectly satisfied God's justice while also displaying His mercy. Because our salvation rests completely on the mercy of God, our love relationship with Him epitomizes everything wrapped up in the word *checed*. Our undeserved and unearned salvation must come by faith alone, trusting in God's mercy by belief in Jesus Christ as our God and Savior. We become justified - meaning declared righteous - "as a gift by His grace through the redemption which is in Christ Jesus" so that God "might be just and the justifier of the one who has faith in Jesus" (Rom. 3:24,26).

The Bible itself represents a wonderful display of God's justice and mercy. Instead of leaving mankind to roam around existentially guessing in spiritual darkness about His will, God went to great lengths to communicate with man. He communicated with us so that He might graciously draw us into an enduring love relationship with Himself. The LORD revealed His existence and divine power through creation, so that with justice no one would have an excuse for rejecting Him. Yet, it took God's special revelation (the Bible) to enable us to fully appreciate His revelation in creation. Psalm 136:1-9 reveals that God made the heavens with skill, spread out the earth above the waters, and made the sun, moon and stars as expressions of His everlasting mercy. The LORD also reveals Himself, His will and His love through men who were carried along by the Holy Spirit. With justice and mercy God had His revelation written down to make it universal and accessible through all generations. The Lord's sovereignty preserved these writings through the ages and His Spirit illuminates them for today's readers.

⁴ George Yancey, "Color Blindness, Political Correctness, or Racial Reconciliation: Christian Ethics and Race," *Christian Ethics Today* (4 Aug 01) 18 Jan 05 http://www.christianethicsto-day.com/Issue/035/Color%20Blindness,%20Political%20Correctness,%20or%20Racial%20Reconciliation%20%20Christian%20Ethics%20and%20Race%20By%20George%20Yancey_035_15_.htm>.

Chapter 16

¹ John Wesley, "John Wesley's Explanatory Notes on the Whole Bible," 13 March 2005 <http://bible.crosswalk.com/Commentaries/WesleysExplanatoryNotes/wes.cgi?book=lu&chapter=010>.

² J. W. McGarvey, Philip Y. Pendleton, *The Fourfold Gospel*, 13 March 2005, <http://bible.crosswalk.com/Commentaries/TheFourfoldGospel/tfg.cgi?book=lu&chapter=010>.

³ Robert Jamieson, A. R. Fausset and David Brown, *Commentary Critical and Explanatory on the Whole Bible*, 13 March 2005 <http://bible.crosswalk.com/Commentaries/JamiesonFaussetBrown/jfb.cgi?book=lu&chapter=010>.

⁴ Tatum, 96.

⁵ Schaeffer, 69.

Chapter 17

¹ Yancey, *One Body One Spirit*, 61.

Chapter 18

[1] Tillapaugh, 137-143.

[2] Tatum, 105.

[3] Diane Cole, "Hooked on the Book," *U.S. News and World Report*, (15 March 2004) 8 August 2004 <http://www.keepmedia.com:Register.do?oliID=225>.

[4] Ralph Neighbour, *Knocking on Doors and Opening Hearts*, (Houston: Touch Outreach Ministries, 1990) 13.

[5] "Project Light: Reading to Build a Relationship" 21 Jan. 05 <http://www.projectlight.org>.

Chapter 19

[1] Alan Flanders, "Press Gangs Were Menace to Townsfolk," *Virginian Pilot*, The Compass, 20 Jan. 05: 3.

Index

Printed in the United States
59089LVS00005B/170

9 780977 618002